D1740541

HD

-5 JAN 2011

1 0 MAR 2011

Suffolk
County Council

Please return/renew this item
by the last date shown.

Suffolk Libraries

www.suffolkcc.gov.uk/libraries/

30127071689066

The Military Error

Baghdad and Beyond in America's War of Choice

Thomas Powers

NEW YORK REVIEW BOOKS

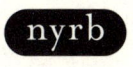

New York

THIS IS A NEW YORK REVIEW BOOK

PUBLISHED BY THE NEW YORK REVIEW OF BOOKS

THE MILITARY ERROR:
BAGHDAD AND BEYOND IN AMERICA'S WAR OF CHOICE
by Thomas Powers

Copyright © 2008 by Thomas Powers

Copyright © 2008 by NYREV, Inc.

All rights reserved.

This edition published in 2008
in the United States of America by
The New York Review of Books
435 Hudson Street
New York, NY 10014
www.nyrb.com

Library of Congress Cataloging-in-Publication Data

Powers, Thomas, 1940 Dec. 12–
    The military error: Baghdad and beyond in America's war of choice / by Thomas Powers.
        p. cm. — (New York Review books collections)
    ISBN 978-1-59017-299-5 (alk. paper)
    1. United States—Politics and government—2001–. 2. Iraq War, 2003—Causes. 3. Iraq
War, 2003—Political aspects. 4. United States. Central Intelligence Agency. 5. Intelligence
service—United States. 6. Weapons of mass destruction—Iraq. 7. Bush, George W. (George
Walker), 1946—Political and social views. 8. Deception—Political aspects—United States.
9. September 11 Terrorist Attacks, 2001—Influence. I. Title.
    E902.P69 2008
    956.7044'3—dc22
                                                                              2008019254

ISBN 978-1-59017-299-5

Printed in the United States of America on acid-free paper.

1 3 5 7 9 10 8 6 4 2

For Bushrod

Let there be no talk of dogs
When wolf and grey-wolf meet.

Suffolk County Council	
07168906	
Askews	Sep-2008
327.730567	£8.99

Contents

Introduction

THE OPTION ON THE TABLE

AT A MOMENT OF SERIOUS CHALLENGE, battered by two wars, ballooning debt, and a faltering economy, the United States appears to have lost its capacity to think clearly. Consider what passes for national discussion on the matter of Iran. The open question is whether the United States should or will attack Iran if it continues to reject American demands to give up uranium enrichment. Ignore for the moment whether the United States has any legal or moral justification for attacking Iran. Set aside the question whether Iran, as Secretary of Defense Robert Gates recently claimed in a speech at West Point, "is hellbent on acquiring nuclear weapons." Focus instead on purely practical questions. By any standards Iran is a tough nut to crack: it is nearly three times the size of Texas, with a population of 70 million and a big income from oil which the world cannot afford to lose. Iran is believed to have the ability to block the Straits of Hormuz in the Persian Gulf through which much of the world's oil must pass on its way to market.

Keep in mind that the rising price of oil already threatens the world's economy. Iran also has a large army and deep ties to the population of Shiite coreligionists next door in Iraq. The American military already has its hands full with a hard-to-manage war in Iraq, and is proposing to send additional combat brigades to deal with a growing insurgency in Afghanistan. And yet with all these sound reasons for avoiding war with Iran, the United States for five years has repeatedly threatened it with military attack. These threats have lately acquired a new edge.

President George W. Bush and Vice President Dick Cheney are the primary authors of these threats, but others join them in proclaiming that "all options" must remain "on the table." The option they wish to emphasize is the option of military attack. The presidential candidates in the middle of this campaign year agree that Iran is a major security threat to the United States. Senator Hillary Clinton in the last days of April threatened to "totally obliterate" Iran—presumably with nuclear weapons—if it attacked Israel. Senator Barack Obama dismissed Clinton's threat as "bluster" in the familiar Bush style but agrees that Iran cannot be permitted to build nuclear weapons, and he too insists that a US attack on Iran is one of the options which must remain "on the table." The presumptive Republican candidate, John McCain, takes a position as unyielding as the president's: Iran must abandon nuclear enrichment, stop "meddling" in Iraq with support for Shiite militias, and stop its sponsorship of "terrorism" carried out by Hezbollah in Lebanon and Hamas in Gaza. Any of these threatening activities, in McCain's view, might justify an attack on Iran.

Sometimes the president's threats are chillingly explicit. In April the administration released details of the intelligence that explained an Israeli air strike last September on a large, blocklike building in which Syria, with the help of North Korea, had allegedly been building a nuclear reactor. Releasing this information, Bush said in April, was Washington's way of "sending a message to Iran and the world for that matter about just how destabilizing nuclear proliferation would be in the Middle East."

The message to Iran was clear—stop or run the risk of a similar attack. Left ambiguous was the question of attack by whom—Israel, which proved itself willing with the attack in Syria, or the United States, which has more planes and missiles at its command? The kind of attack Iran might expect has been spelled out in news stories over the last few years. Some Iranian nuclear research sites are buried as much as seventy meters underground, and there are scores, perhaps hundreds of sites in all, so any serious American effort to destroy Iranian nuclear programs would require intense and numerous strikes by US bombers and missiles. For a time some administration officials lobbied to include the use of nuclear weapons in the strike options for attacking Iran's protected nuclear targets, but vigorous opposition from the Joint Chiefs of Staff scotched that possibility two years ago.

Yet even conventional bombing attacks are acts of war; unprovoked they are acts of aggression. Iran has said it would respond to an attack but without specifying how. Possible counterattacks might target shipping in the Persian Gulf, or US forces in Iraq or Afghanistan, or something else the US has not anticipated. Such an exchange could not long be confined to tit for tat. An all-out American bombing program might force Iran to capitulate, or it might not. The next step would be invasion, destruction of Iran's conventional army, occupation of Iran's capital, and change of Iran's regime, which has long been an openly declared policy objective of the United States.

Is there anyone outside the US government who thinks it makes sense to invite trouble on this scale? Even some insiders are of two minds. "Another war in the Middle East is the last thing we need," Gates said in his speech at West Point, "and, in fact, I believe it would be disastrous on a number of levels. But the military option must be kept on the table."

Forgive me, but why? The military option is a threat; if the threat is carried out it promises widening war and the possibility of failure on the scale of disaster. Why does a policy of courting disaster have to remain on the table?

Nothing in the modern affairs of nations has been more exhaustively analyzed and debated than the utility and dangers of nuclear weapons, and yet the dangers posed by Iran with a bomb have been barely discussed. They are treated as a given. The core idea is that Iran cannot be trusted because the country is run by religious fanatics crazy enough to use a bomb if they had one. This is not the first time such arguments have been made. Some Americans, including Air Force generals, believed in the late 1940s that a preemptive war against the Soviet Union was justified by the peril of Moscow with a bomb. Twenty years later the Russians, in their turn, were so alarmed by the prospect of Beijing with a bomb that they quietly proposed to the Americans a joint effort to destroy the Chinese nuclear development effort with a preemptive attack. The world's experience with nuclear weapons to date has shown that nuclear powers do not use them, and they seriously threaten to use them only to deter attack. Britain, France, Russia, China, Israel, South Africa, India, Pakistan, and North Korea have all acquired nuclear weapons in spite of international opposition. None has behaved recklessly with its new power. What changes is that nuclear powers have to be treated differently; in particular they cannot be casually threatened.

More recently the examples of Iraq and Libya have suggested that international sanctions work more effectively than military threats to persuade nations to give up bomb programs. As is now well known, American fears of Saddam Hussein with a bomb were unfounded. In early 2003, when the US was loudly insisting that only military invasion and regime change could keep Saddam from acquiring a bomb, the United Nations arms inspector Hans Blix said that whether the danger was real or imaginary could be determined by international weapons inspectors in a matter of months. In the event the Americans themselves, after a year spent ransacking Iraq for evidence of nuclear weapons activity, announced that Saddam's bomb program had been completely shut down a dozen years previously, in 1991. But despite the success of sanctions against Iraq the United States continues to speak as if only threats or actual attack might block an Iranian bomb.

Official reluctance to spell out why Iran more than other nations cannot be trusted with a bomb has been matched by reluctance to consider why Tehran might want one in the first place. Iran's nuclear weapons program began under the Shah in the 1970s, sputtered for a time after the revolution, and was then revived after the Persian Gulf war in 1991 which evicted Saddam Hussein from Kuwait. The Iranian government flatly denies that it is pursuing nuclear weapons, hell-bent or otherwise. Recently the CIA released its own conclusion that Tehran had abandoned any formal R&D effort to design nuclear weapons and fit them to a delivery system.

But whether or not that is or remains true is in one sense irrelevant; the hard part—say 90 percent of the challenge—in manufacturing nuclear weapons is making fissionable material, and in that Iran appears to be well on its way to success with its new, more efficient design of centrifuges for uranium enrichment. So set aside the question whether Iran wants an enrichment program to make bomb-grade material or only for the production of electricity; if they get either, they get both. It is a relatively—stress relatively—simple task to turn highly enriched uranium into a weapon. Iran with highly enriched uranium poses almost the same threat as Iran with a bomb. What we ought to ask, then, is why Iran wants its own production capacity for making the stuff of bombs?

What officials say, when they say anything at all, is that Tehran wants a bomb in order to dominate the Persian Gulf region and to threaten its neighbors, especially Israel. This is a misreading of how other nuclear powers have made use of their weapons. As tools of coercive diplomacy nuclear weapons are almost entirely useless, but they are extremely effective in blocking large-scale or regime-threatening attack. There is no evidence that Iran has a different motive, and plenty of reason for Iran to fear that attack is a real possibility.

Indeed, the Bush administration, far from trying to quiet Iran's fears, makes a point of confirming them every few months. These threats are not limited to words, but are supported with practical steps—the presence of large American armies just across Iran's borders in Iraq and Afghanistan, and the dispatch of the world's largest fleet of warships to cruise along Iran's Persian Gulf coastline. The Bush administration further accuses Iran of "meddling" in the affairs of its neighbors, of supplying weapons and training to Iraqis who kill Americans, and of being the world's principal state sponsor of terrorism. Fear that Saddam Hussein might provide nuclear weapons to terrorist groups was the leading American justification for the invasion of Iraq, and the same concern is often cited about Iran.

The seriousness of American threats is confirmed by the fact that no significant national leader in the United States has ever disowned or objected to them in clear, vigorous, principled language. It is as if the whole country listens to the administration's threats with breath held, wondering if Bush and Cheney really mean to do as they say, and in effect leaving the decision entirely to them. Americans may count on the president to think twice, but why would leaders in Tehran, responsible for the lives of 70 million citizens, want to depend on President Bush's restraint for their survival and safety? Bush has a history. On his own authority, without the sanction of any international body, he attacked Iraq five years ago and precipitated a bloody chain of events which shows no sign of abating. It would be natural, indeed inevitable, for any government in Tehran, seeing what has happened next door, to ask what could save Iran from a similar fate. An answer is not far to seek: nuclear weapons with a reliable delivery system could do that.

The continuing military occupation of Iraq, the expansion of military efforts in Afghanistan, the desire to carry the war against the Taliban across the border into Pakistan, and the resort to military threats to force the government of Iran to give up its nuclear programs all represent examples of what has become the American approach during the Bush years to getting what it wants in the world—relying on military force to resolve political problems. How else are we to explain two wars and the threat of a third? Sometime during the Clinton years a faction of the Republican Party in exile lost patience with the accepted way of conducting foreign relations. Talking, negotiating, proposing alternatives, cajoling allies with economic and military aid, taking conflicts to the United Nations, convening conferences, sitting on commissions, and issuing, repeating, and underlining warnings—in short, all the other "options on the table"—came to be seen in certain Republican circles as time-wasting, irresolute, and futile—a pattern of weakness that invites defiance.

The argument of the neoconservatives, stated in its nakedest form at the outset of the Bush administration, notes that the United States is the world's sole great power. We have a military capability that dwarfs all others. We need not defer to weak and corrupt governments that treat us with disdain.

The change was already underway when the shock of the attacks on September 11 created something like a Dirty Harry moment—an abrupt end to patience, a breaking with civility, a rejection of pettifogging legality, a brushing aside of caution in the use of force, all those Aunt Sally hesitations which Secretary of Defense Donald Rumsfeld intended to root out as part of the Pentagon's "old think." The goal was a kind of internal liberation of the national psyche—comfort with the word "imperial," unashamed acceptance of power, eagerness to put boots on the ground, plain talk with anybody who stood in our way, prompt action if they did not step aside. Preemption was the dominant word in the new national security strategy issued in 2002. At West Point that spring the president said, "America will not wait to be attacked again. We will confront emerging threats before they fully materialize." The idea was in effect to clean up Dodge—to stop fooling around, remove defiant regimes, and make the Middle East safe for America and its friends.

Rarely has a theory been quashed by reality more abruptly. Iraq, as we discovered after the capture of Baghdad, had in fact posed no threat whatever, and its occupation brought a host of expensive and intractable new problems which continue to sap American strength. In Afghanistan as well, little went as planned. The Taliban was removed, not destroyed, and gradually it has returned. Pakistan, once a chief American ally in the region, now resists American pressure to pursue the Taliban into Pakistan's tribal areas. In Iraq, most American initiatives in five years of war have had the effect of strengthening the Shiite friends and allies of Iran. The government in Baghdad confers often with Iran, and the influence of Iran is heavily felt in Lebanon and Gaza. Iran dismisses all threats aimed at its nuclear programs as if the United States and Israel were powerless.

With its time in power rapidly running out, the Bush administration is mired in two frustrating wars, stretched thin militarily, living on borrowed money, and exhausted intellectually. It would be hard to name a time when the United States faced a wider range of political problems, or had better reasons to avoid additional military entanglements. Bush and Cheney concede nothing of the kind, but promise "serious consequences" for continued Iranian defiance. It is a strange fact that the locus of opposition to attack on Iran is not in Congress but in the Pentagon, where an insider told the reporter Seymour Hersh two years ago, "There is a war about the war going on inside the building." When the administration planned to add a third aircraft carrier group to the Fifth Fleet in the Persian Gulf, the move was blocked by the then newly promoted chief of Central Command, Admiral William Fallon, who told friends that war with Iran "isn't going to happen on my watch."

Until his resignation in March 2008, Fallon often contradicted and undermined the tough talk of the administration, speaking dismissively about the prospects of war with Iran. "Another war is just not where we want to go," he told the *Financial Times*. "This constant drumbeat of conflict ... is not helpful and not useful," he said to al-Jazeera television. In recent months Fallon also traveled in Afghanistan and spoke at candid length with the military writer Thomas Barnett, who was working on an article for *Esquire*. When the article was ready to go to the printer Fallon invited an *Esquire* photographer to Central Command headquarters in Tampa, Florida, to take his picture. War with Iran, yes or no, Barnett wrote, would "all come down to one man"—Fallon. The White House was not happy with Fallon's interference, Barnett reported. Washington rumor said Fallon's time was short. His removal, Barnett predicted, "may well mean that the president and vice-president intend to take military action against Iran before the end of this year...." A week after Barnett's piece appeared in *Esquire*, Gates announced that Fallon was retiring at his own request. The *Esquire* article had been the talk of the Pentagon nonstop; leaked stories were coming from all directions. Fallon wasn't just on his way out; Gates said he would be gone by the end of the month.

Fallon's open and outspoken resistance to the idea of war with Iran represents something new and extraordinary—maybe. It is too early to be sure. But beneath the surface of recent statements by Fallon, Gates, and the chairman of the Joint Chiefs of Staff, Admiral Mike Mullen, something large seems to be swelling up—resistance by the Pentagon to passive acceptance of a wider war. To see the shape of the conflict one must first accept the seriousness of both parties—the administration in making its threats to stop Iran's nuclear program, and Pentagon officials when they say a wider war would be practically difficult and strategically unnecessary.

This showdown—if it is truly taking place—has been a long time coming. Ten years ago a young Army major, H. R. McMaster, published a history of American escalation of the war in Vietnam, *Dereliction of Duty: Lyndon Johnson, Robert McNamara, the Joint Chiefs of Staff, and the Lies that Led to Vietnam*. McMaster's argument, stripped to its core, was that against their own best judgment the Joint Chiefs passively acquiesced to White House pressure to expand the war. Johnson, with his eye on a second term, did not want to be the first American president to lose a war, and the Joint Chiefs did not want to run their careers aground. Despite the harshness of McMaster's conclusion his book was widely read in the Pentagon and made a deep impression on a generation of rising officers, many of them now of flag rank and in positions of responsibility.[1]

When a reporter asked Gates if Fallon's departure "means we're going to war with Iran," the secretary called the idea "ridiculous." But he didn't leave it at that. He began his own campaign of public remarks stressing the importance of a peaceful resolution of the challenge posed by Iran's nuclear program. As he had at West Point, Gates held fast to the administration's basic stance—"all options are on the table"—but he drained the pugnacity of the claim with Fallon-like flourishes. "We need to figure out a way to develop some leverage... and then sit down and talk with them," Gates said in mid-May. "There is no doubt that...we would be very hard-pressed to fight another major conventional war right now." Admiral Mullen sounded a similar note when he recently told a television journalist in Israel that he was "very hopeful" that the US could avoid a conflict with Iran, which he evaluated as "a very significant challenge." Mullen added, "I certainly share the concern about Iran and about the leadership, and I think it is very important that we increase as much as possible the financial pressure, the diplomatic pressure, the political pressure, and at the same time keep all the military options on the table."

Develop some leverage...sit down and talk...financial pressure, diplomatic pressure, political pressure....

These are unfamiliar words coming from the Bush administration. They roughly echo the approach of Barack Obama, who has said he would "talk" to the leaders of Iran, meaning that he would commence

---

1. McMaster, a 1984 graduate of West Point, went on to distinguish himself in Iraq, where he later served as adviser to the American commander there, General David Petraeus. His name was recently added by Petraeus to an official Army list of nominees for promotion to brigadier general. McMaster is also one of the Army's leading theorists of counterinsurgency.

discussion of serious issues without first demanding concessions. The Bush administration rejects this idea. A few years back, at a moment when Iran still had a relatively moderate president and was prepared to offer major concessions to the US, it refused to talk to Iran at all; now it is prepared to talk, but only after Iran has suspended its uranium enrichment program. The words are slightly altered, but the stance remains intransigent. In his recent speech to the Israeli Knesset, Bush, without naming Obama, denounced his approach as "this foolish delusion," discredited in the 1930s when the British thought they could "talk" to Hitler. In the world according to the neoconservatives no failing of character is more craven or pusillanimous than a willingness to talk to fascists, Nazis, or dictators. Bush plunged the rhetorical knife in deep: "We have an obligation to call this what it is—the false comfort of appeasement."

Bush and Cheney prefer the language of flat command that implies "or else." A long list might be appended here of their frequent warnings that the United States does not trust Iran with the knowledge to enrich bomb-grade uranium and will not tolerate an Iranian bomb. Many of these warnings have been issued in the last month or two and we may expect a continuing barrage until their final days in office. The president's frustration is plainly evident: Saddam Hussein may be gone, but Iran remains defiant, and more powerful than ever. The president's male pride seems to have been aroused; he said he was going to solve the Iranian problem and he doesn't want to back down. The intensity of Bush's desire to crush this final opponent is evident in his words and his body language, but does he retain the power to carry out his threats?

From one point of view the answer seems obvious. It is too late. With the exception only of the neoconservative faithful, every close observer of the American-Iranian standoff says that the administration's threats are empty, that the United States does not have the military resources, or the political support at home, or the agreement of allies abroad, to carry out a full-scale air attack on Iran's nuclear infrastructure, much less to invade and occupy the country. Two of the skeptics, Gates and Mullen, are running the Pentagon, and their cautioning remarks, only a step this side of insubordination, would seem to make attack impossible. But if attack is impossible, why does Bush talk himself into an ever-tighter corner by continuing to issue threats? Does he believe Iran will cave? Are these the only words he thinks people will still listen to? Is he hoping to tie the hands of the next president? Or is he preparing to summon the power of his office to carry out the last option on the table? One hardly knows whether to take the question seriously. It seems alarmist and overexcited even to pose it when the realities are so clear. But it is impossible to be sure—Bush has a history.

The articles included in this collection were all (but one) written for *The New York Review of Books*. With the exception of this introduction they are printed here in chronological order, oldest first. Only very minor changes have been made to the text to reflect the passage of time—insertion of a date, for example, to replace the words "recently" or "last fall," etc. These essays represent my effort to understand what was happening as events were unfolding, driven by decisions which were reached in extreme secrecy. An earlier collection of similar material, *Intelligence Wars: American Secret History from Hitler to al-Qaeda*, was published in hardcover in 2002, and in paperback the next year with several additional pieces about the beginning of the war in Iraq. One of those pieces, "War and its Consequences," published at the outset of the war in March 2003, helps to explain what has most preoccupied me ever since—the danger that the war would spread to engulf the region. That article concludes:

> But a war to overthrow Saddam Hussein won't by itself provide a "decision outcome" in the present case because there are two

rogue states with programs to build nuclear weapons in the Middle East. The theory says that both have to go, and if President Bush can be taken at his word, he thinks the same thing. To me, the implication seems clear: Iraq first, Iran next.

We're not free of this danger yet.

Thomas Powers
June 1, 2008

I

THE FAILURE

THIS IS A MOMENT OF CRISIS for the Central Intelligence Agency—the second in the half-century since it was established in 1948 primarily to serve the president. Directors of central intelligence are now confirmed by the Senate before they can take office, and they are required to report on their activities in a timely manner to the intelligence committees in Congress, but these gestures of oversight and restraint have not limited the power of presidents to use the CIA as they see fit. In past decades presidents have used the CIA to carry out acts of war against foreign nations, to attempt to assassinate foreign leaders, to raise funds in order to conduct secret wars, and even, in the notorious instance called Watergate, to attempt to quash the FBI's investigation of a White House–directed burglary team. The current crisis is the result of a White House–directed campaign to justify the overthrow of Saddam Hussein by citing intelligence reports of Iraqi stockpiles of weapons of mass destruction and accelerating programs to build more. But following the fall of Baghdad a CIA team more than a thousand-strong failed to find any WMD stockpiles, and the team's director, David Kay, concluded after six months of fieldwork that Iraq's research-and-development programs had been suspended or shut down years earlier.

This apparent failure of American intelligence is the subject of several ongoing investigations and is bound to be a matter of controversy for years to come. The failure is compounded by what Kay's team actually found—empty warehouses, idle factories and laboratories, as well as clear evidence that the regime in its last years had been corrupt, demoralized, and disintegrating. The CIA, it appears, was not only ignorant of the true state of affairs in Baghdad, where imaginary WMD "programs" were used to extract large sums from an increasingly erratic Saddam Hussein, but the agency's estimating arm in October 2002 had also expressed "high confidence" in a frightening list of allegedly real and present dangers that simply did not exist. Public controversy and congressional investigators have understandably focused on these twin failures. How could the CIA, with a budget in the many billions and a total staff approaching 20,000, get things so badly wrong? But two separate questions, in my opinion ultimately more important, have for the moment been skirted by observers and investigators alike: Did the CIA director, George Tenet, and other high agency officials respond to White House pressure for estimates that would support the administration's determination to go to war? Did the administration intend from the beginning to use these alarming intelligence reports as a blunt instrument to extract a vote for war in Congress?

The war in Iraq is described as an "entirely irrelevant military adventure" by Richard A. Clarke, a career government official in charge of White House efforts to fight terror under both President Clinton and President Bush. In his book charging that the Bush administration was slow to grasp the threat posed by Osama bin Laden, *Against All Enemies,*[1] Clarke writes that President Bush made a bad situation immeasureably worse by his "unprovoked invasion" of Iraq, taking the United States down "a path that weakened us and strengthened the next generation of al Qaedas."

The most troubling question raised by Clarke is how the CIA, which warned the Bush White House urgently and often of an

---

1. *Against All Enemies: Inside America's War on Terror* (Free Press, 2004).

impending terror attack over the summer of 2001, could have followed that professional triumph with repeated and explicit claims to
have found Iraqi weapons of mass destruction which weren't there.
Clarke's answer ought to give every American pause. The day after al-
Qaeda's devastating attacks on the Pentagon and the World Trade
Center, Clarke says he "walked into a series of discussions about Iraq"
in the White House, which were not about "getting al-Qaeda." Instead
"I realized with almost a sharp physical pain that Rumsfeld and Wolfowitz were going to try to take advantage of this national tragedy to
promote their agenda about Iraq." The implication is clear: "getting
Iraq," in Rumsfeld's words, came first, followed many months later, in
the fall of 2002, by the CIA's evidence of weapons of mass destruction.

Investigating the origins of the Iraq war is certain to be awkward
and painful but, taken seriously, it promises to teach Americans much
about two kinds of danger that intelligence organizations pose to the
nations that employ them. One is obvious and well understood by
everybody—getting important things wrong. In its first half-century
the CIA got lots of things wrong. In 1948 it was much criticized for
failing to predict a coup in Columbia that resulted in a civil war that
has still not ended. In 1950 it failed to foresee intervention by the Chinese in the Korean War, a mistake that almost resulted in American
armies being driven entirely from the peninsula. In 1968 the agency
was surprised by the Russian invasion of Czechoslovakia, a failure
repeated in 1979 when the agency failed to predict the Russian invasion of Afghanistan. Ten years after that the estimators continued to
issue new alarms about Soviet power and intentions almost until the
very moment the Berlin Wall came down, signaling the true end of
the cold war, an event soon followed by a still greater astonishment—
the actual collapse and breakup of the Soviet Union itself.

None of these failures was followed by a catastrophe on the
ghastly scale of Pearl Harbor, and I believe all were honest—based on
genuine misreading of the tea leaves. It is not hard to identify things

bound to happen, but it is very hard to say when. The CIA has long struggled with the difficulty of forecasting but has never found a good way to estimate the probability of the awful things everybody fears. Estimators have learned to choose caution and qualification as the wisest course, despite the inevitability of occasional mistakes. On the long list of horrors that might happen, after all, some will.

A second kind of danger posed by intelligence organizations is both harder to prove and, especially in a democracy, harder to admit— their exploitation by the executive branch of government as tools of domestic coercion and control. President Richard Nixon always believed that the CIA had a liberal bias and deliberately fed information to John F. Kennedy, which helped him to win the 1960 presidential election. I have never seen evidence that it really happened but that does not mean Nixon was wrong. A clearer example can be found in the summer of 1964, when the administration of President Lyndon Johnson authorized the CIA to run aggressive over-the-beach operations to land South Vietnamese sabotage teams in North Vietnam while American destroyers patrolled nearby in the Gulf of Tonkin. North Vietnamese patrol boats may have attacked the destroyers one night early in August; a second attack was almost certainly imaginary but was nonetheless cited as justification for an American air raid on North Vietnam, and used to push through a hasty congressional resolution later cited by President Johnson as authority for the war in Vietnam.

Calling them as they see them is the official governing ethic of the CIA, and for the most part that is what the agency does. But the CIA works for the White House in the same way that the Defense Intelligence Agency works for the secretary of defense, and no one who read DIA estimates of Soviet missile programs throughout the cold war ever doubted for a minute that "the threat" would always justify buying, building, or developing whatever the secretary of defense had on his wish list. Can giving higher-ups what they want be called dishonest if it's inevitable?

A long book might be written on this subject, but for our purposes here it is enough to say that no one can understand, much less predict, the behavior of the CIA who does not understand that the agency works for the president. I know of no exceptions to this general rule. In practice it means that in the end the CIA will always bend to the wishes of the president, and as long as the director of central intelligence serves at the pleasure of the president this will continue to be the case. The general rule applies to both intelligence and operations: what the CIA says, as well as what it does, will shape itself over time to what the president wants. When presidents don't like what they are being told they ignore it. When they want something done they press until it happens. As a disciplined organization the agency does not complain about the one, or long resist the other. In a word, it is responsive.

Understanding this general rule opens a useful window onto American behavior in the world. Presidents generally make no secret of what's on their minds—Kennedy loudly worried about Fidel Castro's plan to export the Cuban revolution in the 1960s, Nixon and Reagan urgently warned of Soviet missile-building in the 1970s and 1980s, Bush worries openly about Iranian efforts to develop atomic bombs now. Knowing what's item number one on the agency's agenda is readily learned from what presidents and their advisers say, a street that runs both ways: if you know what the CIA is doing, you know what the president wants done.

Once put into words the general rule seems obvious. Why would the CIA ignore what the president wants or believes? Why would a president tolerate a CIA with an agenda of its own? But at times the general rule leads to troubling questions of the sort democracies hate. In the 1980s it was learned that the CIA was actively supporting contra forces in Nicaragua in flagrant violation of a congressional ban. The general rule would say that President Reagan not only knew of the effort but authorized and directed it. Who else? But this obvious conclusion was evaded by the special prosecutor, Lawrence Walsh, and congressional investigators, and historians generally have consigned "the Iran-contra affair" to the dark attic of American history reserved for awkward questions labeled by tacit agreement as too difficult to unravel. Architects of the CIA anticipated such awkward moments by establishing a policy of "plausible deniability"—organizing "sensitive" secret operations at one remove from the White House so presidents might "plausibly deny" having authorized or even known about any that are publicly revealed. There have been plenty of occasions for denial over the years, but claims that the White House was out of the loop, while routinely accepted, are rarely plausible.

The challenge facing investigators now, and historians later, is to explain how the evidence of Iraqi weapons of mass destruction collected by the CIA—wrong in almost every instance—was used by President Bush and his principal advisers to describe an urgent and growing danger which justified a preemptive war. Can the White House plausibly claim that its loud misreading of the evidence was not driven by a determination to go to war? Can the president plausibly claim that the war policy was not his, or that he did not know he and his spokesmen were exaggerating the dangers they cited? It is these questions which define the crisis confronting the CIA—an increasingly clear-eyed skepticism among legislators, commentators, the broad general public, and the rest of the world that American intelligence officials, when they are under pressure, can be trusted to call them as they see them. Down this road the questions get harder, not easier, because distrust of the CIA must soon expand to include first the president's advisers, and finally the president himself.

The first time a Senate investigating committee seriously looked into the way presidents use the CIA was in 1975, following discovery by the public that the CIA had made serious and sustained efforts to assassinate Cuba's Communist leader, Fidel Castro. The existence of the plots raised the obvious question: Who authorized them? Efforts to kill Castro had begun under President Eisenhower, were actively pursued under President Kennedy, and were not abandoned until after the election of President Johnson in 1964. It was not only presidents and their defenders who denied that the White House had plotted murder; the chief of the CIA during the years when the plotting was at its height, John McCone, also insisted he knew nothing of these schemes and as a Catholic would never have agreed to them. At the outset of the investigation the committee's chairman, Senator Frank Church of Idaho, in effect accepted these denials at face value and said he thought the CIA had behaved like "a rogue elephant on a rampage" during the years when Castro's overthrow was a principal goal of American foreign policy. A "rogue elephant," of course, listens to no one.

But all talk of a "rogue" CIA had disappeared before the Senate investigating committee finally published its 350-page report, *Alleged Assassination Plots Involving Foreign Leaders*, in November 1975. This extraordinary document recounted in meticulous detail the CIA's many attempts, some with the help of notorious Mafia gangsters, to kill Castro, along with its involvement in other plots to kill Rafael Trujillo in the Dominican Republic, Patrice Lumumba in the Congo, and Salvador Allende in Chile. The Church Committee report was unprecedented; no other nation had ever conducted a comparable investigation of its own intelligence activities, and the report's release was preceded by intense behind-the-scenes maneuvering. An increasingly alarmed President Ford, horrified as news of the plots leaked out during the months of the committee's investigation, reversed his initial support for an inquiry and urged members of Church's committee to keep their findings under wraps.

The pressure was so great that the Senate itself, fearful of taking a stand, refused either to support or oppose publication of the report.

In the end committee members agreed to go ahead only after Senator Church threatened to resign in protest if they repudiated their own work. The result when the report appeared was a predictable nine-day-wonder in the news media and something like a crash course in political realism for reporters, scholars, historians, and the general public. In the past, when American officials had stoutly denied that the United States would ever stoop to secret murder, outsiders could never be really sure if they were being told the truth or a fairy tale. The Church Committee report introduced all who cared to know to the secret world as it is.

But what about the awkward question of authorization—did Presidents Eisenhower, Kennedy, and Johnson approve the murder plots or not? The general rule leaves no room for doubt on this score; of course authority came from the White House—where else? Laymen need not agonize over this question; the absence of an explosion of official anger at the discovery of murder plots provides all the evidence anybody really needs.

The Church Committee did not have the ordinary citizen's luxury of addressing this question on the merits. The defenders of presidents were ready for a bare-knuckle fight to the death, and of course the surviving evidence was never quite 1,000 percent conclusive. Senator Church was a political man in a political town. What to do? In this painful situation the testimony of Robert McNamara unexpectedly offered the Church Committee and its chairman a soft resolution of their dilemma. As the secretary of defense under Kennedy, McNamara was in the government's innermost circle—not just intimately familiar with efforts to overthrow Castro but to some degree even their author. If anyone knew who gave the go-ahead it was McNamara, but he circled the matter with great care. He told the Church Committee that White House approval of assassination attempts would have been "totally inconsistent with everything I know about" President Kennedy and his brother Bobby, who had been placed in charge of efforts to get rid of Castro after the failure of the CIA-backed invasion of Cuba at the Bay of Pigs in April 1961. At the same time, McNamara told the committee, he knew the CIA well—the agency would never go off on its own. He wasn't denying that the efforts to kill Castro took place, he wasn't saying that those efforts were duly authorized, and he wasn't saying that the CIA was out of control. "I understand the contradiction that this carries with respect to the facts," he concluded. The McNamara formula was intellectually weak but it offered a way out. Church accordingly chose caution over glory, followed McNamara's lead, and said in effect that the committee had been unable to establish exactly who authorized the plots.

The failure of Senate investigators, journalists, and historians to identify and hold to account those ultimately responsible for the plots to kill Castro and similar "excesses" of the 1960s—the presidents for whom the CIA worked—has been damaging to the agency, which naturally felt it had been chastised for doing its job. It is not hard to see why presidents like pushing the blame for folly or failure onto others; the puzzle is why those who ought to be paying attention—politicians, journalists, and historians alike—have let them get away with it. In the investigation of Watergate the Senate and House both focused on "the cover-up" and sidestepped the more alarming crimes—the pressure of the Nixon White House on the CIA to assist the White House plumbers in what turned out to be illegal break-ins, and, later, to block the FBI's investigation. Much the same happened during the Iran-contra investigation, when CIA officers faced jail and crippling legal fees while the man in charge of these illegal foreign adventures, President Reagan, was allowed to plead a lapse of memory.

This pattern of blaming the CIA for what presidents have ordered it to do is the single most important cause of the emergence within the agency of a "risk-averse" culture—a learned caution about undertaking operations of the sort CIA officers have later been required to explain or deny under oath on the witness stand. Secretary of State Madeleine Albright once told Richard Clarke that it was not hard to explain the passive-aggressive behavior of the CIA. "It has battered child syndrome." The agency's operational timidity beginning in the mid-1980s is one reason efforts to kill or kidnap Osama bin Laden failed in the years leading up to September 11—a reluctance to act frequently cited by Clarke in *Against All Enemies*. But Clarke credits the CIA with issuing frequent urgent warnings over the summer of 2001, and reserves his most pointed criticism for two failures of the Bush White House—its inability to grasp the urgency of the danger posed by al-Qaeda before September 11, and its folly later in going to war with Iraq. Clarke's strongest passages are reserved for the consequences of this mistake, which diverted American resources and the attention of the White House from the real threat, al-Qaeda, at the very moment when victory in Afghanistan offered an opportunity to deal the terrorist organization a fatal blow. Instead, while the Bush administration busied itself going to war to "disarm Saddam Hussein," al-Qaeda was given a year to recover, reorganize, and carry out many new acts of terrorism. But it appears that the established pattern is repeating itself in the investigation of the CIA's alleged intelligence "failure" while the White House fixation on Iraq, vividly described by Clarke, is ignored.

The investigators will find the going routine so long as they limit their inquiry to the nuts and bolts of intelligence collection and estimate-writing. The CIA, the NSA, and other agencies will grumble about threats to "sources and methods" when they are asked to deliver raw intelligence reports, but some sort of secure procedure will be worked out and investigators will soon find themselves wading through a sea of paper. Technical experts will explain how to read overhead photos or monitor cell-phone traffic with watchwords. Specialists will line up to say why they thought tractor-trailers discovered in northern Iraq after the war were, or were not, mobile biological weapons laboratories. Other specialists will do the same for the now-notorious aluminum tubes which maybe were, but probably weren't, intended for an Iraqi centrifuge. Estimate writers will explain the deliberative process that went into creating the October 2002 Special National Intelligence Estimate (SNIE) on Iraqi weapons of mass destruction, and why the CIA had high confidence that they posed a growing threat, but low confidence that it could predict what Saddam Hussein would do with the weapons.

Much time will be required for this investigation; White House and CIA officials will concede nothing; the issues will be factually complex; long hours of testimony will be delivered in sentences with many clauses; there will be much talk of fragmentary evidence, ambiguous reports, making the most of what you've got, doing the best you can. At day's end, described in a fat report, this exercise may be expected to reveal "an honest mistake"—a picture of the world that, despite expensive hardware, thousands of man-hours, and painstaking debate, turned out to be wrong. Things that looked clear in the beginning will look fuzzy by the end. Appended to the report will be numerous recommendations for new tables of organization, improvements in procedure, more emphasis on training, and of course additional funds.

But this kind of nuts-and-bolts effort will avoid all the really troubling and difficult questions raised by the use of intelligence to convince Congress to vote for an unnecessary war in order to pursue an undeclared policy that the legislators did not understand, much less have an opportunity to debate. I do not mean to imply that the administration's policy had sinister aims; I take the president at his word when he says his purpose was to make America safer. But questions of war and peace affect the whole country, the Constitution specifically provides for the deliberation of Congress, and nothing in the enabling legislation of the CIA suggests that the president alone, and not the Congress, should enjoy the benefit of the CIA's best efforts. The debate is supposed to be honest, but in this case the debate fell short of the ideal by a country mile. To ignore the administration's manipulation of intelligence is to issue an invitation for more of the same.

Investigators will need no instruction in how to conduct a nuts-and-bolts study of the Iraq intelligence failures, and politics will certainly impede and possibly preclude entirely an effort to explain the deeper reasons why and how false intelligence was used to prepare the way for war. But perhaps not. To be serious and complete, investigations now underway, and additional efforts undertaken by historians later, should explore the following questions:

1. The close cooperation between American and British intelligence services which helped President Bush and Prime Minister Tony Blair make their case for war while protecting them from awkward questions. In particular investigators should look into the source and vetting of fabricated documents suggesting that Iraq was trying to buy Niger yellowcake; British claims that they possessed "other" evidence of the yellowcake purchase; the provision to Secretary of State Colin Powell of an allegedly official British report on Iraqi intelligence organizations that was cited by Powell at the UN only two days before journalists revealed that the report was based on materials plagiarized from open sources; CIA collaboration with British intelligence officials in creating an intelligence dossier outlining al-Qaeda responsibility for the attacks of September 11; the content of all communications between British and American intelligence figures in the months between President Bush's appearance before the United Nations in September 2002 and the outbreak of war the following March; and British and American cooperation in espionage targeted on UN Secretary General Kofi Annan and members of the UN Security Council.

2. Communications with the CIA by officials in the Pentagon, the office of the vice-president, and the National Security Council that might have been intended, or reasonably interpreted, as pressure to

skew intelligence estimates. A special office to "re-look" intelligence on Iraq was established in the Pentagon immediately after September 11 by Douglas J. Feith, the undersecretary of defense for policy. This group received numerous reports about Iraqi weapons of mass destruction from Ahmed Chalabi's Iraqi National Congress, which was supported and paid by the Department of Defense. Investigators should track the circulation of these reports, most later dismissed as false or even fabricated, to determine if they were "stove-piped" (a term for sending reports directly to higher-ups without benefit of analysis) to Secretary of Defense Donald Rumsfeld, Secretary of State Colin Powell (who may have depended on them for passages in his address to the UN on February 5, 2003), or NSC staffers who worked on speeches for the president.

3. The origin of the obsession with Iraq which the Bush administration brought into office in January 2001, an obsession well documented in Clarke's book, in the recent book about former Secretary of the Treasury Paul O'Neill, *The Price of Loyalty*; in Bob Woodward's book of 2002, *Bush at War*; and in a second Woodward book, *Plan of Attack*. Clarke describes the obsession with Iraq as "an idée fixe, a rigid belief, received wisdom, a decision already made" eight months before the attacks of September 11. Still missing from the public record is any reliable account of why the administration was already determined to invade Iraq when it had barely heard of Osama bin Laden or al-Qaeda; why it chose to divert attention and resources from Afghanistan while bin Laden and leading members of the Taliban government were still at large, in order to invade Iraq; when and why it chose to justify war by citing Iraq's weapons of mass destruction, how and when the decision for war was discussed with allies, especially Britain; and what the administration hoped to achieve by the conquest of Iraq. It is this obsession with Iraq which best explains the pressure on the CIA to "find" an extensive WMD program which did not exist.

Attempts to answer these questions will be resisted by the White House principally on the grounds of executive privilege, and by the CIA citing its historic understanding with British intelligence that neither will share information received from the other without its prior agreement, which the British may confidently be expected to refuse. No other administration has held its deliberations on sensitive questions more closely, and it is possible that official investigators, journalists, and historians will never really get a full understanding of the purposes and hopes of the president and his advisers as they prepared for war. But the need to explain what happened is made urgent by the now-unmistakable collapse of the official case justifying the invasion. Only one of two things could have happened—either the CIA completely misread the evidence and precipitated an unnecessary war, or the administration determined on war for reasons of its own and insisted that the CIA cobble together a best case from scraps of information in the intelligence grab bag. No official body will decide to state the choices quite this starkly, and the writers of reports will be even less willing to identify the implications. But something went terribly wrong as America debated the need for war in 2003, and each of the possible explanations raises grave questions of trust—either the CIA cannot be trusted to see the difference between real and imaginary dangers, or the agency made itself pliant and supine in the hands of the president, who exploited the CIA to make his case for war.

—*The New York Review of Books*, April 29, 2004

2

HOW BUSH GOT IT WRONG

NO TYRANNICAL FATHER presiding over an intimidated household was ever tiptoed around with greater caution than is the figure of President George W. Bush in the Senate Intelligence Committee's fat report of its investigation into the scary stories about Saddam Hussein's weapons of mass destruction cited by the President as all the justification he needed for going to war in Iraq.[1]

Before the war the CIA expressed "high confidence" that once American soldiers had the run of Iraq they would find stockpiles of chemical and biological weapons, mobile laboratories to make more, vigorous programs to buy uranium and develop atomic bombs, and much else confronting the United States with a "gathering threat" or "growing danger"—words used by the president and other high administration officials to summarize the intelligence laid out in a National Intelligence Estimate (NIE) issued by the CIA on October 1, 2002. Only a week later the dangers described in the NIE convinced Congress to vote for war, and in March 2003 President Bush ordered an invasion of Iraq to remove those dangers once and for all. There would have been no Senate investigation and no report if the

---

1. The Senate Select Committee on Intelligence, *Report on the US Intelligence Community's Prewar Intelligence Assessments on Iraq*, July 7, 2004.

weapons had been found—indeed, almost any one of them would have satisfied—but a year of looking has turned up nothing.

It is presidents, not secret intelligence organizations, who decide if and when the United States shall go to war, but that fact was set aside, perhaps only temporarily, by the Senate Select Committee on Intelligence at the outset of its investigation into the CIA's embarrassing failure to be right about almost anything when it came to Iraq. It is unlikely that most Americans grasp the magnitude of the failure even now, but plenty of others around the world see it only too plainly. France, Germany, and Russia all resisted the American insistence on war in the Security Council of the United Nations, arguing that UN inspectors should be given additional weeks or months to continue their search for these weapons of mass destruction before war could be justified.

American officials and private citizens alike derided their concerns, ascribing them to naiveté, greed, or hatred of America. France in particular was held up to scorn. In the eighteen months following the invasion no one representing the United States—certainly not the president—has apologized for the administration's arrogant insistence that it knew best, or even granted that in retrospect the French, the Germans, and the Russians might have had a point. But those who were proved right—Chirac, Schröder, and Putin—have said nothing triumphant or wounding about the weapons that weren't there, perhaps because they share the Senate Intelligence Committee's cautious restraint when it comes to the office of the president of the United States. More time for inspections might have allowed passions to cool, but the president was impatient, he was tired of "swatting flies," as National Security Adviser Condoleezza Rice later told the 9/11 Commission; and he put the presidential thumb on the scales for war.

Leaving out the president himself has become something of a pattern. The report of the 9/11 Commission, also released in July, is equally circumspect. The names of President Bush and his chief advisers are frequently mentioned, but the idea that the president himself might or should have done something to prevent the terrorist attacks of September 11 is not directly addressed.[2] About as close to actual criticism as the commissioners were willing to go is the flat remark that despite numerous warnings from the CIA, America's

> domestic agencies never mobilized in response to the threat. They did not have direction, and did not have a plan to institute. The borders were not hardened. Transportations systems were not fortified. Electronic surveillance was not targeted against a domestic threat. State and local law enforcement were not marshaled to augment the FBI's efforts. The public was not warned.

These things that were not done must have been not done by somebody, but that somebody, and the somebodies reporting to him, are not criticized by name, although knowledgeable readers who closely read the text get the drift easily enough. The Senate Intelligence Committee has gone the 9/11 Commission one better, barely mentioning the White House or its chief occupant at all. If presidents bear some responsibility for the performance of the directors of central intelligence who report to them, you won't find it in the Senate report on the CIA's biggest misreading of what would be found when the troops went in since it assured President John F. Kennedy in 1961 that rebel guerrillas would be met on the beaches at the Bay of Pigs by wildly cheering Cubans eager to be freed of Castro. Not even the Democratic nominee for president, Senator John Kerry, seems ready to say plainly that this immense mistake—the bloody invasion of Iraq to end threats which have turned out to be entirely imaginary—must

---

2. See the review of the commission's report by Elizabeth Drew in *The New York Review of Books*, September 23, 2004.

properly be tracked to the door of the White House. Virtually all commentators in public office, Kerry included, prefer to linger on the "intelligence failure" itself—the CIA's hundred-page NIE, wrong in almost every particular, and most dramatically about those in which it expressed "high confidence."

But it is too soon for President Bush to hazard a sigh of relief, because the committee plans a second report, scheduled to be completed in 2005, which will address additional questions including "whether public statements, reports, and testimony regarding Iraq by US Government officials . . . were substantiated by intelligence information." Put another way, the question is whether the president and his chief advisers in the run-up to war exaggerated, misrepresented, or ran on beyond the intelligence claims now shown to have been wrong.

There can be little doubt that the outcome of the election in November will affect the tone, perhaps even the conclusions themselves, in this "second phase" of the committee's work. But in going about its work the Senate Intelligence Committee has laid the ground carefully for tough questions to follow, by choosing an unexpectedly narrow question to begin: Did the findings of the CIA in the National Intelligence Estimate of October 2002 rise plausibly from the evidence the agency had to work with? The temptation to score cheap points by matching up predicted stockpiles with the empty warehouses actually found has been firmly resisted by the committee. The estimate is treated on the CIA's own professional terms: Were they wrong but reasonable in their assessments, or did they have to stretch the evidence to be wrong? In almost every case the Senate investigators tell us that the findings—those "high confidence" predictions about what Saddam Hussein had or was trying to get—did not reflect the evidence.

The basic sin came in many varieties—ignoring evidence, misrepresenting evidence, exaggerating evidence, overstating the evidence, going beyond the evidence, interpreting some evidence as strong when it was weak, sometimes even reaching conclusions without any real evidence at all. The report reaches 117 separate conclusions about the October 2002 NIE and other matters relating to prewar intelligence about Iraq, and it is fair to say that almost every one contains a more or less stinging rebuke of the CIA. The report does not say, but unmistakably implies with persuasive detail, that the exaggerations, overstatements, and misreadings of the CIA's estimate writers all fail in one direction—describing Iraq as more dangerous than it really was.

Now why was that? you ask. The committee did too. In 2003 the chairman, Senator Pat Roberts, said he was "concerned by the number of anonymous officials that have been speaking to the press alleging that they were pressured by Administration officials to skew their analysis, a most serious charge and allegation that must be cleared up." In a secret committee hearing with leading intelligence officials on June 19, 2003, Roberts repeated his concerns and asked for help:

> Did any of you ever feel pressure or influence to make your judgement...conform to the policies of this or previous administrations? The second part of that is, has any analyst come to you or expressed to you that he or she felt pressure to alter any assessment of intelligence? And finally, if you did feel pressure or were informed that someone else felt pressure, were any intelligence assessments changed as a result of that pressure?

Even before the war Washington was afloat in rumors that intelligence about Iraq was being skewed, but details were hard to pin down. Late in 2003 the journalist James Bamford, best known for his books about the National Security Agency, was told by a CIA officer working on intelligence about Iraqi WMDs that "I never saw anything" proving Saddam had or was developing weapons of mass destruction, and "no one else there did either."[3] Office wisdom within the agency said the cupboard was bare. But in late 2002, while UN inspectors were reporting from Iraq that they had found no prohibited weapons or programs, the administration was pushing hard to build its case that Saddam's WMDs were reason for war.

On December 21, according to Bob Woodward in his book *Plan of Attack*, George Tenet arrived at the White House with John McLaughlin, a career intelligence analyst who had risen to become the CIA's deputy director, to outline the case for WMDs. It was a briefing in the classic mode of the sort sometimes called a dog and pony show—slides and flip charts about missile payloads and ranges; reports of bulldozer activity that suggested efforts to hide chemical or biological weapons programs; an elegant technical argument proving that Saddam was flight-testing an unmanned aerial vehicle with a range three times the distance permitted under UN rules; defector reports about mobile laboratories that could be used to brew up terrible diseases; recordings of Iraqi military officers apparently engaged in efforts to hide things from UN inspectors.

Many of the charges outlined by McLaughlin were later cited by Secretary of State Colin Powell in his speech to the United Nations on February 5, 2003, laying out the administration's case for war. But Powell, who got mainly rave notices at the time, evidently has a gift for expression not shared by McLaughlin. At the White House briefing on December 21 the president was unimpressed. "This is the best we've got?" Bush asked Tenet, according to Woodward. "George, how confident are you?" "Don't worry," said Tenet, in a remark widely quoted, "it's a slam dunk."

Exactly what Tenet intended to convey by that remark is unknown; he declined to own or deny it.[4] But the effect was a whirlwind shaking

3. See Arthur Schlesinger's review of Bamford's book *A Pretext for War: 9/11, Iraq, and the Abuse of America's Intelligence Agencies* (Doubleday, 2004) in *The New York Review of Books*, September 23, 2004.

4. Until the publication of his own memoir; see "What Tenet Knew," p. 101 in the present volume.

of the cupboard in the CIA office charged with tracking Saddam's WMDs, the Weapons Intelligence, Nonproliferation and Arms Control Center, referred to by its acronym, WINPAC. It was in this office that Bamford's informant worked at the turn of the year 2002–2003. In January the informant's boss at WINPAC convened about fifty people in a meeting to bolster the case for WMDs, described by Bamford in *A Pretext for War*. "And he said, 'You know what—if Bush wants to go to war, it's your job to give him a reason to do so.'"

Thoroughly disgusted, Bamford's informant quit WINPAC but moved on to another intelligence office where he continues to do roughly the same work. It is probable that Senator Pat Roberts's invitation to whistle-blowers reached the ears of Bamford's informant but he did not choose to repeat to the Senate Intelligence Committee the marching orders issued by his boss at WINPAC. In her testimony, Jami Miscik, the agency's chief of intelligence analysis, admitted there was a lot of interaction of CIA officials with policymakers, including Vice President Dick Cheney "coming back to certain points or issues repeatedly...." Cheney crossed the Potomac to discuss WMDs at the CIA as many as eight times in the year before the war, and Miscik conceded that an analyst pressed to go over and over some point about Saddam's nuclear weapons program, say, "might be able to say or might think of that as some sort of, if not pressure, then some sort of a reluctance to accept the answer they were given...."

But was there outright pressure to change an assessment? No one claimed anything quite like that, despite a platoon of witnesses asked to identify anything—anything—that smacked of White House pressure. In its report the committee quoted eight analysts who went beyond the typical "no" or "never" when they were asked about pressure from on high. Among their comments:

- "...It might be that our assessments suited what they needed.

But we were never pressured to make an assessment a certain way or anything." (Biological weapons analyst at the CIA)

• "I did not have any analysts come to me [to say] they were feeling pressure to change their judgments...as far as I'm concerned, there were no such things happening." (National intelligence officer for science and technology at the CIA)

• "We had no internal or external influences on what [the analysts'] judgments were." (Chief of programs on nuclear weapons at the Defense Intelligence Agency)

• "I think the NIE...was a rushed process like we talked about, but as it stands our position is adequately represented in there." (Nuclear weapons analyst at the Department of Energy)

About as close to charges of actual skewing as the committee could find came from two former intelligence officials, Gregory Thielmann, who left his position as head of the State Department's Bureau of Intelligence and Research (INR) shortly before the NIE was written, and Richard Kerr, a retired CIA official called back by Tenet to review the Iraqi WMD intelligence once it was clear the inspectors had come up empty. Kerr said that some CIA analysts had complained of the repeated questions from White House and other high officials, but in his opinion "nobody changed a judgment" and in any event "it is not at all unusual for analysts to feel they are being pushed by one group or another." Not even Gregory Thielmann, who had publicly criticized the Bush administration for building its case on "faith-based intelligence," said he could provide the names of specific analysts who had altered specific assessments under pressure. In its report the committee said it "did not find any evidence" that Cheney or other administration officials tried to coerce analysts.

I am not surprised. Asking CIA analysts if they have been cooking the books while their bosses sit in the room reminds me of those well-meaning Western lefties who paid visits in the 1930s to prisoners in the Soviet gulag and returned with assurances that the prisoners all agreed the food was great and they were getting plenty of outdoor exercise. Understanding how the CIA came up with its "high confidence" NIE requires the Senate to connect the dots, but it shouldn't be hard. There are only two—the White House and the CIA. Which way does the committee think the influence runs? But the Senate Intelligence Committee has declined to hazard a guess on this point, and its careful wording amounts at best to a Scotch verdict—not proven. But the rest of the report, with its numerous examples and close analysis of evidence used to build a case for war, raises troubling questions about the CIA's ability to dig in its heels when a president insists that a grab bag of ambiguous information is all he needs to prove a "gathering threat" or a "growing danger."

The one danger that trumped all others was the atomic bomb—"the smoking gun that could come in the form of a mushroom cloud," as Bush put it in a speech in Ohio on October 7, 2002. That turn of phrase has an interesting history recounted by Bamford in *A Pretext for War* and by Michael Massing in *The New York Review of Books*.[5] It first appeared in a story by Judith Miller and Michael Gordon in *The New York Times* on Sunday, September 8, a month before the President's speech in Ohio. Miller and Gordon reported that Saddam Hussein's Iraq "has stepped up its quest for nuclear weapons," a claim proved by its efforts to buy "specially designed aluminum tubes, which American officials believe were intended as components of centrifuges to enrich uranium." One official was quoted anonymously as saying that "the first sign of a 'smoking gun'... may be a mushroom cloud." As it

---

5. "Now They Tell Us," *The New York Review of Books*, February 26, 2004.

23

happened Secretary of Defense Donald Rumsfeld, Vice President Dick Cheney, and National Security Adviser Condoleezza Rice all appeared that Sunday on talk shows to warn of the very danger that Miller and Gorden had reported—Saddam with a bomb. "We don't want the smoking gun to be a mushroom cloud," said Rice on CNN.

The president's Ohio speech came a week after the CIA published its NIE, formally titled *Iraq's Continuing Program for Weapons of Mass Destruction.* If Bush had sound reason to warn of mushroom clouds he must have found it in the NIE. Accordingly, the Senate Intelligence Committee devoted 106 pages of its 529-page report to the evidence provided by the CIA to back its "high confidence" that Iraq was "continuing and in some areas expanding" its nuclear program, that it could build a bomb "in months to a year" once it had the fissionable material, and that "we are not detecting" all of Iraq's efforts to acquire nuclear weapons. Details aside, that roughly adds up to a claim that the prospect of Saddam armed with a bomb was definitely a "gathering threat." What the Senate Intelligence Committee did was to ask whether the CIA and other intelligence organizations who contributed to the writing of the NIE actually had evidence to support their conclusions.

The heart of the agency's case was built around four factual claims —that Iraq was trying to buy a kind of uranium ore called yellowcake in Niger; that Iraq was trying to buy thousands of aluminum tubes that could be used as rotors in a centrifuge to separate fissionable material; that magnets, high-speed balancing machines, and machine tools on the Iraqi shopping list were intended for its bomb program; and that Saddam himself was taking a personal interest in the program and in the community of scientists who were running it. In every case the Senate committee found that the evidence for these claims was thin or nonexistent, and it strongly suggested that the CIA's analysts and estimate writers consistently ignored or dismissed evidence that undermined or contradicted their central claims.

The CIA's bedrock assumption that Saddam never abandoned his hope of developing nuclear weapons can be traced back to the shock of discovering just how close he had come before the invasion of Kuwait in 1990. The cease-fire that ended the first Gulf War in early 1991 provided for open-ended inspections by the United Nations to confirm Saddam's promise that he would shut down his weapons programs and destroy stockpiles of prohibited items. The Iraqi nuclear establishment that was discovered and dismantled during these inspections showed that Iraq might have been as little as a year away from producing a working atomic bomb. Saddam Hussein's continuing defiance convinced the CIA and just about every other intelligence organization paying attention that Iraq might be down, in the WMD game, but it was not out.

The sanctions then imposed on Iraq made any all-out effort impossible but the CIA assumed that once the sanctions were ended Saddam would resume his race for a bomb. It was a reasonable assumption, just as it was reasonable to reconsider the assumption after the UN inspectors left Iraq in 1998 and conclude he wouldn't wait till sanctions were removed—the inspectors' departure offered Iraq all the freedom it needed to get going. But reasonable assumptions do not a proof make and the actual evidence assembled by the CIA and its rival in the Pentagon, the Defense Intelligence Agency (DIA), was in fact shaky, beginning with the CIA's claim in the NIE that Iraq had been "vigorously trying to procure uranium ore and yellowcake."

The case of the Niger yellowcake has already been explored in public, but the Senate Intelligence Committee adds significant detail to the story, stressing that the yellowcake was the only item on the Iraq shopping list that did not have a dual use—i.e., it could not be used for civilian as well as military purposes—thereby lending it additional strength as evidence. The report that Iraq had approached Niger to discuss a yellowcake purchase came originally from the British, but when the CIA sent former ambassador Joseph Wilson to

Niger to check it out, he said that none of his contacts confirmed it. He added that the Niger uranium mines were operated by the French, and it would be all but impossible for five hundred tons of yellowcake to be diverted to Iraq.

Wilson's report, according to the committee, was never circulated to the White House or cited in intelligence estimates; nor were later reports from a US diplomat in Niger discounting the yellowcake claim, and another State Department eyes-on check of a warehouse in which the US Navy had reported the yellowcake was being stored. The checker found only bales of cotton. Nevertheless, the British repeated the claim in a "white paper" issued on September 24, 2002, and an early draft of the president's Ohio speech contained a reference, eventually dropped, to the yellowcake buy. An NSC staffer, according to the Senate's report, initially resisted CIA advice to drop the claim because it would leave the British "flapping in the wind." Even the CIA's John Mclaughlin stepped back from the British white paper in a congressional hearing when he said, "I think they stretched a little bit" in pressing the yellowcake claim.

But the yellowcake story refused to die. A sheaf of fabricated documents arrived from Italy to muddy the waters in October 2002 and the president included the yellowcake story in his State of the Union address in January—the soon-to-be-exploded sixteen words that "the British government has learned that Saddam Hussein recently sought significant quantities of uranium from Africa." But despite the potential significance of the new documents, which purported to record the yellowcake deal, the CIA made little effort to obtain copies of their own, and when they did they were sluggish in checking them for authenticity despite a warning from the State Department's Bureau of Intelligence and Research saying they looked fishy.

Eventually the documents were shared with the International Atomic Energy Agency, which reported almost immediately that the documents were crude and obvious forgeries, a conclusion with which the CIA was subsequently compelled sheepishly to agree. This summary only sketches in lightly the many ways in which the CIA over a period of months demonstrated the faintest sort of desire to know whether Iraq was really trying to buy yellowcake or not. In favor of the story are vague rumors and unsubstantiated claims; against it were many specific denials, and yet this gossamer web of "evidence" was pumped up in the NIE to support a claim that Iraq was "vigorously" seeking new sources of uranium. The CIA did not make up or fabricate the yellowcake story, but the Senate report clearly shows, although it is too polite to say, that the agency estimators fabricated the "vigor" that was nailed on to give the claim weight and urgency.

The only other concrete things cited as evidence of Iraq's determination to build nuclear weapons were the aluminum tubes which it was allegedly trying to buy, apparently from China. The tubes were real enough, and Iraq's desire to buy them has not been questioned either. But what were the tubes for? On that question the Senate committee found that intelligence estimators had divided into two camps—those (mainly in the CIA and DIA) who believed they were intended for use in a centrifuge, where over the course of a year they might be used to separate enough uranium-235 to make two atomic bombs; and those (mainly in the Department of Energy and the State Department's INR) who believed that the technical characteristics of the tubes, the history of Iraqi use of such tubes for missiles, and the Iraqi claims that the tubes were in fact intended for use in missiles all proved that the tubes, although prohibited by UN sanctions, were not part of Iraq's nuclear program, if indeed it had one.

The Department of Energy in particular argued in great detail that the tubes were all wrong for uranium enrichment, and Iraq's past efforts at a centrifuge program had followed a different path. One DOE analyst said, "We should just give them the tubes." But the CIA ignored these doubts, sought "expert" advice backing the centrifuge interpretation from outside contractors who did not know enough to disagree, exaggerated the cost of the tubes, accepted a single flimsy claim that Saddam was "closely following" the tube purchase, falsely claimed that "almost every country" approached by Iraq to build the tubes said the tolerance specifications were too high, and while citing a DOE-INR "footnote" of disagreement in the text of the NIE, put the actual text of the footnote sixty pages deeper into the paper.

The committee's report faults the CIA in every one of its twenty conclusions about analysis of Iraq's nuclear program. It builds an argument for finding that the agency's crafting and shaping of the NIE can only be described as an attempt to manufacture a case justifying war. But this case, if the committee should ultimately decide to dot the *i*'s and cross the *t*'s and state it plainly, must await the convening of a new Congress after November's election.

Despite the committee's reluctance to accept the logic of its own report, it is already clear that the agency's false, exaggerated, and overstated claims set the stage for war. In December 2002 the CIA was asked to write an official evaluation of Iraq's *Currently Accurate, Full and Complete Disclosure* of its weapons programs—a 12,000-page document delivered to the UN inspectors as required by the Security Council's Resolution 1441, which sent inspectors back into Iraq and started the countdown to war. Woodward devotes a long section of *Plan of Attack* to the inclusion of this requirement in Resolution 1441. Vice President Dick Cheney argued that the *Full and Complete Disclosure* was the poisoned apple which would bring down Saddam Hussein, since he could never comply honestly with the demand. Either he would lie about what he had in late 2002, or he would admit he had been lying about WMDs for years past. "That would be sufficient cause to say he's lied again," Cheney said, according to Woodward, "he's not come clean and you'd find material breach and away you'd go," i.e., to war.

In the event the French successfully insisted on wording the resolution to say that a "material breach" would require a false declaration and a general failure to cooperate. But the distinction was empty; lies in the declaration, plus Iraqi failure to help the UN inspectors find the truth, would constitute the double-fault justifying war, and it was in that spirit that the CIA pounced on the *Full and Complete Disclosure* as soon as it was released by the Iraqi government in Baghdad on December 7. We learn from the Select Committee report that while WINPAC at the agency wrote the response, two analysts at INR and DOE, disgruntled at being shut out of the drafting process, exchanged complaints by e-mail. "It is most disturbing," the DOE analyst wrote,

> that WINPAC is essentially directing foreign policy in this matter. There are some very strong points to be made in respect to Iraq's arrogant non-compliance with UN sanctions. However, when individuals attempt to convert those "strong statements" into the "knock out" punch, the Administration will ultimately look foolish—i.e., the tubes and Niger!

Now, nearly two years later, it is abundantly clear that the many claims made by the White House about "the tubes and Niger" were either substantially or completely wrong. But whether these errors were genuinely "foolish" depends on knowing what the false claims about Iraqi WMDs were intended to achieve. In October 2002 the claims were scary enough to win a vote by Congress for war. At the turn of the year they were used again to bolster the American case that Saddam couldn't be trusted, and military action alone could solve the problem. The CIA-written *US Analysis of Iraq's Declaration* was unequivocal: Saddam Hussein was defying the UN's Resolution 1441 and was in noncompliance because Iraq in its declaration

fails to acknowledge or explain procurement of high specifica-
tion aluminum tubes...[and] fails to acknowledge efforts to
procure uranium from Niger....

The French, Germans, and Russians, as well as Hans Blix, continued to argue that the inspectors should be given more time, but no
one came to the defense of Iraq's *Full and Complete Disclosure*; no
one said its "failure" to acknowledge current WMDs may well have
been accurate. Wrong as they were, the CIA's claims about Iraqi
WMDs held up long enough to do what the president wanted—provide a reason for going to war.

Americans are quick to criticize presidents for everything they don't
like, or want but don't have, and at times they are willing to harass
them so unmercifully on irrelevant personal grounds that presidents
may be forgiven for regretting they were ever elected in the first place.
But when it comes to the really big mistakes and disasters in public
life, Americans can be strangely reluctant to hold presidents responsible. This reluctance can be seen plainly in discussion of the two recent
intelligence failures—"catastrophic" in the words of a *New York
Times* editorial on August 11, 2004—that are cited as the reason for
fixing a badly broken system: the "failure" to predict and prevent the
terrorist attacks of September 11, 2001, and the "failure" in predicting
discovery of Iraqi weapons programs that turned out to be imaginary.
George Tenet, before he retired as director of central intelligence,
presided over both failures and is widely blamed for the faltering
management that allowed them to happen, but while Tenet will have
much to explain if he chooses to write a memoir, neither of these two
failures can be usefully laid at his door. Consider first the report of the
9/11 Commission, which recounts in great detail the numerous ways
in which the CIA and the FBI failed to grasp essential details and connections in the al-Qaeda plot to strike at America. There is a kind of

agony in reliving the near misses by investigators who might have put it all together in time. Small wonder that the 9/11 Commission, and now Congress, are determined to oil the machinery so it will never happen again. But the 9/11 Commission also described in detail things that worked right, and no part of its report deserves closer scrutiny than Chapter Eight—"The System was Blinking Red"— which recounts the numerous warnings issued by the CIA in the year leading up to September 11.

"Warnings and indications" have always been the first priority of the CIA. The agency was created in 1947 specifically to prevent another disaster on the scale of Pearl Harbor, and its history can be read as a continuing saga of dangers spotted or missed—the successes so often, and fairly, described as unsung, and the failures which generate storms of criticism and typically leave the agency battered and gun-shy.

Throughout the cold war defectors and spies handled by the CIA were always asked first, before anything else, if they knew of any imminent threat to or attack planned against the United States. In the first half of 1961 none of the persons interrogated at the agency's Defector Reception Center in Frankfurt, Germany, reported anything of the kind. Nor did they describe what many had seen—huge stockpiles of building materials in Berlin—because questions about such preparations weren't high on the list. The result that summer was a painful and potentially dangerous surprise when the Soviet Union suddenly divided the city of Berlin with a wall—a huge construction project requiring vast stores of cinder block and barbed wire which the Soviets had accumulated under the agency's eyes. Thereafter new questions were added to the debriefing of defectors, having to do with unusual East Bloc activities that might not appear threatening at first glance, but could provide clues to dangers around the next turn in the road.

During the hearings conducted by the 9/11 Commission Condoleezza Rice and other witnesses for the administration frequently said that the CIA never gave them a warning they could act on—a name, an address, an airline flight number, a city, a specific plan and time of attack. President Bush added that he would have moved heaven and earth to protect America if only someone had told him what needed to be done. But just how much detail did he really need? According to the 9/11 Commission's report, before September 11 the Presidential Daily Brief (PDB) which the CIA delivered every morning to the White House included "more than 40" articles "related to Bin Laden."

In March 2001 Richard Clarke, chief of the counterterrorism staff in the National Security Council, advised Rice against reopening Pennsylvania Avenue to traffic passing in front of the White House, warning that al-Qaeda cells were operating inside the United States and truck bombs were among their weapons of choice. In May the chief of the CIA's Counter-Terrorism Center, Cofer Black, warned Rice that the threat level was close to the level it had reached during the millennium, when major plots were thwarted in Jordan and in the United States, including one targeted on Los Angeles International Airport. On June 25, Clarke cited six separate reports of al-Qaeda plotting; three days later he added that terrorist activity "had reached a crescendo." At the same time the CIA was instructing all station chiefs to warn host governments around the world and to seek their help in disrupting terrorist cells. On June 30 an agency briefing was headlined "Bin Laden Planning High Profile Attacks."

So it went, day after day, week after week. By late July, George Tenet told the commission, the threat level could not "get any worse" —"the system was blinking red." This appears to have been the case in both senses. The collection efforts of the CIA and other organizations were not only bombarded with signs and reports of threatening activity, but the warning system itself—all those channels of communication intended to rouse the president and the White House staff to alarm and activity—was "blinking red." This gale-force wind of warning reached its highest level on August 6, when the PDB delivered to President Bush on vacation in Texas was headlined "Bin Laden

Determined to Strike in US." For two years the White House fought to suppress the text of that warning and it is not hard to see why. It contains no addresses, dates, names of visa violators—no "actionable intelligence," as Rice has frequently pleaded in the president's defense. But the stark fact of Osama bin Laden's desire to strike hard at the United States burns through unmistakably.

Hijacked planes, Osama's knowledge of the millennium attack planned for Los Angeles airport, his patient planning for years before operations are carried out, the existence of seventy FBI field investigations of al-Qaeda activity inside the United States, even a reminder of the 1993 attack on the World Trade Center—it would be hard to imagine the system blinking red more vividly than it does in the PDB of August 6. One can imagine the terrible frustration of George Tenet over the following two years, criticized for "failing" to prevent the attacks on September 11, and forbidden by circumstance and loyalty to the president from bursting out with the obvious question—what more did he need?

But like the Senate Intelligence Committee, the 9/11 Commission stops there. Perhaps holding presidents accountable is more than any commission or Senate committee can fairly be asked to do; perhaps only the electorate can properly hold a president accountable. We shall see.

But it is clear that no attempt to fix the system can hope to succeed if it cannot or will not identify the part that is broken. Warnings are useless, if a president will not listen. No attempt to assess a foreign threat can hope to be accurate if the estimators answer directly to the White House, are in effect part of the president's team, have been told unmistakably what the president wants, and know full well that their careers will flower or wither under his hot breath. Journalists and members of Congress know how this works; for the most part they went along as well.

The Senate Intelligence Committee is scheduled to deliver in 2005 its final verdict on the CIA's National Intelligence Estimate used to justify war. It has stated in its July 2004 report that the estimate writers went beyond the intelligence they had to work with, and it will probably say as much about the president and other high officials who went further still in banging the drum—citing "gathering threats" and "growing dangers" that not even the most liberal of readings could find in the NIE. But taking the final step—stating plainly what is obvious to anyone who cares to see—may be more than the Senate Intelligence Committee, or any other group of official Americans, can bring itself to do.

The big idea on the table for fixing intelligence at the moment is the proposal, formally put by the 9/11 Commission, to establish a "national intelligence director" who will crack the whip when the dozen or so American intelligence organizations drag their feet, resist cooperation, insist on going their own way, cannot agree who is to run the spies, hold on to secrets too tightly or too loosely, or squabble over division of the immense, $30–40 billion American intelligence pie. This is a workable idea that will step on many toes but only one set of toes will really count. The Department of Defense may be expected to resist bitterly any loss of its control of intelligence budgeting, but it is ultimately presidents who will decide. President Bush has adopted the words but seeks to avoid the essence of the 9/11 Commission's proposal; he would welcome a national intelligence director, but seeks to retain direct White House control of the director of central intelligence, who is the person who makes or breaks careers at the CIA, and ensures that the agency remains in effect an arm of the White House. It is that relationship—the intimate partnership between president and DCI—which explains why the CIA turned a miscellany of iffy intelligence reports into "high confidence" warnings of Iraqi WMDs.

If things had been otherwise, if the CIA had pressed and bullied the White House instead of the other way around, then the President would have lashed out angrily when the inspectors found nothing, and it became apparent that he had taken the nation to war without cause. But nothing of the kind happened. President Bush was serene.

For a year he said those weapons might yet turn up, and Tenet loyally said the same. When others suggested something had gone badly wrong, the president expressed confidence in his director of central intelligence, just as he had following the attacks on September 11, and for the same reason. The country didn't know it then, and the White House did what it could to keep the country from ever knowing, but for seven months George Tenet's CIA had been hand-delivering warnings to the president about al-Qaeda at a rate of nearly two a week. Tenet might have volunteered one or two additional pieces of information—for example, the report he received on August 23 that FBI field agents in Minneapolis wanted to investigate an "Islamic extremist" arrested while learning to fly 747 airliners. Tenet says he told the White House nothing about that. It sounds odd, but that is what Tenet says. With that exception, Tenet's performance as DCI was everything this president could ask for, and every word from Bush on the subject so far suggests that he agrees.

This is where things grow difficult for committees, commissioners, and ordinary citizens alike. It is not sympathy for President Bush as a person that makes them hesitate, but the power of the office of the presidency itself. A president is not only the leader of the country, but the leader of his party as well, and a serious attack on a president concerning a substantial matter is an invitation to conflict of a kind that resembles civil war. So the reason for the velvet gloves with which he is treated is not hard to understand. But the failure to act before September 11 and the unnecessary war with Iraq cannot fairly be blamed on intelligence organizations or anyone else. The White House is the problem, not for the first time. Iraq is President Bush's war. He insisted on it, and nothing can save us from the same again until we find the will to hold the president responsible.

—*The New York Review of Books*, September 23, 2004

3

THE ELECTION AND
AMERICA'S FUTURE

THE BIG ISSUE IN 2004 is Iraq—will voters reject President Bush's invasion and occupation of Iraq, or will they accept and endorse it by giving him a second term? This question is not complicated, and the answer either way will be clear and crushing. Bush's defeat will signal to the world, and to the Republican Party, that the president's decision for war has been rejected by the country as unjustified and unwise. Bush's victory will signal something roughly the opposite—that the country has accepted and endorsed his decision, thereby transforming Bush's war into America's war.

Many other questions will of course be answered at the same time, but the question of Iraq is the one that will have the greatest consequences, because it will have the most to do with how long the war lasts. Mainstream thinking about this war has come a long way since Congress and just about everybody else accepted President Bush's claim that Saddam Hussein had and was seeking weapons of mass destruction and that this posed a "growing danger" for the United States. But mainstream thinking may not be ready to accept a conclusion that this war, like the intervention in Somalia at one end of the spectrum of pain, or like Vietnam at the other, will be seen in retrospect as a failure. How big a failure, after how much pain, waits on events.

My reasons for thinking the war will end in failure are not compli-cated either. To me, it seems the inevitable consequence of attacking a country that posed no threat, of trying to create a government of our choosing for people we do not like or understand, of defining those who fight back as terrorists, and of ignoring the elementary fact of war that killing people makes enemies of their relatives, friends, and neighbors. How many Iraqis have we killed so far? Ten thousand? Fifty thousand? Is anyone keeping count?

From the day Saddam Hussein disappeared in Baghdad nothing has gone as the administration expected, and our ability to manage the chaos has grown steadily weaker. In the end the Iraqis will decide what comes next, but not until they have fought it out, and that will be impossible until we quit interfering. When is that likely to happen? Not while Bush remains in office, and I suspect that his successor—Kerry next year or somebody else in 2009—will also find it hard to face up to the failure, but will go on from month to month and year to year hoping that a little more blood and sacrifice will make it all come right. But maybe not. Maybe this time around a quick, harsh dose of pain and failure will be enough to bring a halt.

If President Bush were defensive about his failure in Iraq, Ameri-can voters might feel safer in calling him to account, but he is not defensive. He is so self-assured, defiant, and determined, and those waging his campaign are so aggressive and insulting in their attacks on Kerry personally, that voters are in danger of being swept away by the drama of the president's defiance. This High Noon brand of politics is apparently the brainchild of Bush's chief political adviser, Karl Rove. The idea is to raise the temperature of campaign rhetoric beyond norms of civility, in the hope of driving all the thousand important public issues into the background, and thereby forcing vot-ers to see, and compelling them to accept or reject, only the image of the grinning Texan standing tall in his shirtsleeves, spitting on his hands, and challenging the flip-flopper, as he challenges the world, to step up or run home to mama. Some might describe Rove's High Noon politics as the gamble of a desperate campaign running on empty, but Rove could quote H. L. Mencken in defense, who said that no man ever lost a nickel by underestimating the intelligence of the American people.

Victory by such means, on a matter of such consequence, is a troubling prospect. But I do not think that voters on election day will forget everything else—the failure to restore lost jobs, a ballooning of the national debt that threatens Social Security, the watering down or outright repeal of regulations on business and the environment, the failure to fund the No Child Left Behind Act, the spreading loss of health benefits for ordinary Americans, above all the blunder of the unnecessary war. I can't think of any significant category of voters won over by Bush since he squeaked through in 2000, and I can't see why the country would vote for more of the same. So I think that Rove's gamble will flicker briefly in the polls before sputtering out, and that Bush will lose.

That is what I think. But what I fear is that a different dynamic is at work—that voters may share a gut sense that the Iraq adventure will end in failure, but are too angry and distracted to admit it, want to feel good about High Noon America for a few moments longer, and will vote for Bush in order to put off the inevitable bitter day.

—*The New York Review of Books*, November 4, 2004

4

SECRET INTELLIGENCE
AND THE 'WAR ON TERROR'

NOW IS A GOOD TIME for Americans to pause and consider our progress in what the Bush administration chooses to call the war on terror. Osama bin Laden remains at large three years after the attacks of September 11, the war in Iraq has reached a kind of stasis of escalating violence matched by an erosion of our ability to control events there, new crises loom with other members of the "axis of evil" defined by President Bush in January 2002, and the president's reelection rules out the likelihood of any sudden change in American policy. With suspense on that point ended for the moment, we ought to weigh what we have learned from the linked disasters of September 11 and the war in Iraq, and what we should fear or expect next as American plans and facts on the ground sort themselves out in the Middle East.

The Central Intelligence Agency finds itself at the center of this unfolding story in a way we have come to expect from its conflicted history as a tool of the White House and as the nation's principal collector and analyst of secret information. The CIA is not only deeply involved in the day-to-day fighting of the war on terror, but is simultaneously charged with knowing, and with telling those who have a need to know, who our enemies are, what dangers they pose, whether American efforts are working, and how other governments react to what we are doing. Intelligence is a function of the executive branch of government and as such it answers to the president—just as the Bureau of Labor Statistics and the United States Forestry Service do. Like them it is supposed to serve the nation as a whole, but like them it can also be used by the White House to help the president politically—in the case of the CIA, generally by controlling the flow of information to ensure that good news reaches the public while bad news remains secret, compartmented, and codeword-protected beyond the scrutiny of Congress and public alike.

A kind of rough etiquette has evolved around this fact of life— presidents are granted a lot of latitude when it comes to classifying information, but they cross the line when they use the CIA directly against political opponents, as Richard Nixon did during the Watergate episode; or when they use the CIA to do secretly what Congress has forbidden, as Ronald Reagan did during the Iran-contra affair; or when they suborn the CIA to exaggerate, distort, or misrepresent intelligence findings, as I believe the White House of George Bush did during the run-up to the Iraq war. The reports of the CIA's Iraq Survey Group and the Senate Intelligence Committee do not reach but lend support to this conclusion and thus invite us to consider again, as previous reports have done, the difficulties encountered by democratic governments when they grant national leaders more or less unsupervised control over secret intelligence services.

What we have learned from the history of the CIA is that it is subject to extraordinary internal stresses whenever American presidents encounter unexpected challenge or failure abroad. Past agonies are captured in a string of names, each in its own way a rich mosaic of illusion and failure—Cuba, Vietnam, Iran, Nicaragua—and it is already clear that Iraq must be added to that list. Indeed it is my guess that Iraq will be cited as the outstanding object lesson for decades to come of the ways in which evidence can be tortured to justify what presidents want to do. It is a tossup whether the president or the agency will be blamed once the dust has settled. But if history is our guide we must expect the CIA to take the fall, and it is not yet clear whether it will survive this latest trauma, or in what form.

The fate of the agency is no minor matter to intelligence professionals who have spent their careers trying to serve both presidents and the nation; all know that these two masters are often at odds, and many have been forced to hire lawyers, face grand juries, and risk jail for what they did, or for failing to describe truthfully what they did, for presidents unable or unwilling to take the stand themselves. There is no easy way to reconcile these divided loyalties. But there are good reasons for trying to understand what has now brought the stresses to the breaking point, especially for the analytical side of the CIA. Put simply, President Bush has laid an immense wager that the American military invasion and occupation of Iraq will result in a stable government friendly to the West and thereby make America safer. Some members of the administration have argued further that a genuine democracy in Iraq will help to change the political landscape in the Middle East, and Paul Wolfowitz, one of the Pentagon architects of the plan to invade Iraq, was even quoted as saying before the war that the road to Jerusalem—by which he meant peace between Israel and the Palestinians—lay through Baghdad.

These hopes seem to have dimmed now, but the wager is on the table and cannot be withdrawn. Social and political realities in the region of conflict will determine whether the answer is win, lose, or draw, but CIA analysts, drawing on the resources of all American intelligence organizations, will be the first to know how things are going, just as they had the deepest knowledge of the dangers before the war. George Tenet, who resigned as director of central intelligence in July 2004, always insisted that the analysts call them as they see them, but that gets progressively harder to do as the president, with his policy on the line, makes it understood what he is expecting to hear. That's where the stress lies—in the crack of daylight between White House hopes and reality on the ground. The wider the crack the greater the stress.

In the nine months before September 11 the White House officer charged with worrying about terrorism, Richard Clarke, found it impossible to get the full attention of high officials with warnings about al-Qaeda because the administration had a different agenda in mind—building a super-expensive, space-based anti-missile defense system. Critics of the Bush version of the Star Wars plan said the reasons for that had died with the cold war; terrorism was the danger facing America in the first years of the twenty-first century. The 9/11 Commission reported that Clarke, the CIA, and others had warned the administration as many as forty times of the threat posed by Osama bin Laden, but that is not what the administration wanted to hear, and it did not hear it.

In the months before the war in Iraq the crack opened again; Bush and Vice President Dick Cheney insisted that Saddam Hussein's weapons of mass destruction posed a "gathering threat" and a "growing danger." The evidence was spotty and inconclusive, but the National Intelligence Council still managed to give Congress an estimate stressing the dangers with "high confidence." The crack of daylight is now plainly visible following Bush's wager as insurgency widens in Iraq. The president insists that "freedom is on the march" while as I write thousands of Marines have been fighting their way into the resistance-dominated city of Falluja—a large-scale set-piece battle eighteen months after Bush, thumbs up in a flight suit, proclaimed an end to "major combat operations" on the deck of a US aircraft carrier under a banner reading "Mission Accomplished."

Nothing in Iraq has so far gone the way Bush and his advisers predicted. What is new is the level of stress placed on American intelligence analysts now, torn between reality and official optimism, raising the necessary question whether the analysts can be trusted to do their work honestly by what we might call the ancillary consumers of intelligence—not only Congress, which has some legal right to know what the CIA is doing and saying, but also the press and television, the general public, and the whole rest of the world, which includes the intelligence services of America's coalition partners and traditional allies. Ancillary consumers have limited access to American intelligence product but they get the general drift of what the CIA is saying in the manner of any alert reader of newspapers over time, and their support for American policy depends in part on their confidence that the people down in the boiler room trying to make sense of events have access to timely and accurate information, understand the region, know what the administration is trying to do, and are telling the president what they really think—in other words, calling them as they see them.

For the broader world watching the unfolding drama of the war on terror, or any other great American initiative abroad, we might say that the CIA serves in some ways as the canary in the coal mine—when it shows sign of stress, we know something is wrong either with intelligence collection or with the policies it is intended to support. It's always one or the other—the evidence is thin or missing, or it points to conclusions that meet resistance. A classic early example was the American reliance in the 1960s and 1970s on the heavy and relentless bombing of North Vietnam and the supply trails south through Laos and Cambodia to break the will of Hanoi and win the war for our side. Increasingly throughout the Vietnam War CIA estimators spoke in a strange croak—everybody wanted to know if the end was in sight but so far as I know the agency delivered its opinion on everything but, and never reported in plain language that the strategy was working—or not working.

Instead, for nearly ten years, the estimators who monitored Operation Rolling Thunder focused on trying to measure the pain—so many trucks, so many men, so many dollar-equivalents in munitions fed into the top of the funnel to get one fifth, or one tenth, or one hundredth that amount out the bottom to carry on the war. At that time Americans were still learning how to eavesdrop on the intelligence world and never fully understood the stress the CIA was under to deliver good news, or to conceal the bad news by ever-tighter focus on the minutiae of evidence. Still, everybody paying attention got the drift. Presidents and their advisers might insist the bombing campaign was working to shorten and win the war, but the war itself refuted them.

Bad as the stress got to be during the Vietnam War years, it is worse now. We might say that after failing to find Saddam Hussein's weapons of mass destruction the canary fell insensible from its perch—a second unmistakable sign that things are seriously awry. The first, of course, was the finding of the 9/11 Commission that American intelligence, despite its vast capacity to monitor the world, failed to prevent the destruction of the World Trade Center on September 11, 2001. But the second, parsed in detail by the Senate Intelligence Committee and more recently in the report of the Iraq Survey Group, recounted in detail how intelligence analysts managed to misread the crippled and demoralized dictatorship of Saddam Hussein's Iraq as a vital state building weapons of mass destruction which posed a "gathering threat" for the West. What brings any student of intelligence to a kind of shocked halt is the fact that CIA analysts did not get anything right—every claim about Saddam's WMDs was wrong—completely wrong, flatly wrong, wrong by a country mile.

We have already heard much about these two failures, and it is perhaps time to move beyond the failures of the past in order to anticipate potential future failures while there is still time to do something about them. But that effort will be helped by a brief description of what the linked failures of September 11 and Iraq seem to me actually to represent—in the first case, a classic example of the CIA falling on its sword so the White House might "plausibly deny" responsibility for something which had gone badly wrong. Serious professional lapses by the agency, the FBI, and others before September 11 have been identified, principally holding on to information that should have been shared, or ignoring warnings from the field when they reached the upper ranks. But too little in my opinion has been said about what the CIA and Richard Clarke in the White House both got right—the numerous warnings delivered to the president and his national security advisers. Condoleezza Rice has said that these warnings were too vague and the president has said that he would have moved heaven and earth if he had only known when and where the terrorists planned to attack. The White House was paralyzed, the official version goes, because the intelligence organizations of the United States had failed to connect the dots....

But the fact is that the intelligence analysts who provided warnings to the White House connected a great many dots—they anticipated the use of commercial aircraft, they knew that al-Qaeda cells were operating inside the United States, they knew that Ramzi Yusef, the field commander of the first attack on the World Trade Center in 1993, had hoped to bring the towers down, and had promised an FBI debriefer after his arrest that another attempt would be made. They knew that al-Qaeda wanted to strike inside the United States, and they knew that al-Qaeda was approaching the operational climax of a new effort. In a sense all the most important dots had been loosely connected except for the last two or three.

The question then is whether an alert administration, anxious to protect the country, knew enough to do something—to give a dynamite charge to intelligence chiefs, or summon the officials responsible for public safety and disaster relief, or prod the Federal Aviation Administration to beef up security at airline gates, or ask the Immigration and Naturalization Service if borders were secure, or suggest to the FBI that suspected terrorist cells should be put on notice that they were being watched. Best might have been an attempt to put all those officials in a windowless room for a day with orders to report to the president personally before the sun went down. Presidents do not normally find it hard to get the attention of government offices, and bureaucrats all know how to put on a show of frantic activity. That, at the very least, is what we should have found when the lights went on after the attacks of September 11.

This is not a stretch. I don't think I am being unfair. Think of the battery of big storms which hit Florida in 2004.[1] Every one was anticipated vigorously despite the fact that it was impossible to say precisely when or where the heart of the storm would strike until the final hours. If you wait, it's too late. So the authorities evacuated the Keys—unnecessarily. They evacuated New Orleans—unnecessarily. But they put all the responders on alert, and they evacuated coastlines which in fact were hit, and bad as the storms were, they might have been a great deal worse if everybody had sat back and waited for the connecting of the final dots on the weather map. The same response might have been given to the CIA's warnings before September 11. There are lots of things to do when you don't know exactly what to do. But the president did nothing. It would be hard to find words adequate to describe the full range and amplitude of the nothing that he did. My own preliminary, working explanation is that for reasons of his own the president decided to do nothing. Why? Historians will be occupied for many years before they come to agreement on the answer to that question.

But the United States is a forgiving country when it comes to presidents, and it is the American intelligence community—not the president or the White House—which has been the object of righteous anger for the "failure" of September 11.

Much the same is the case with the missing Iraqi weapons of mass destruction. Predicted stockpiles of chemical and biological weapons were not found after the fall of Baghdad because they did not exist. For more than a year the White House insisted it was too early to

---

1. The authorities were less alert the following year when Katrina hit New Orleans. The Bush administration never foresaw a genuine danger.

confess failure—the weapons themselves or a hidden infrastructure for their development and construction might still turn up. The psychology of this official reluctance to admit failure is not hard to understand. It is unlikely that the United States had ever been more comprehensively and significantly wrong about anything, ever, than it was in identifying the reasons for going to war in Iraq.

But why did the director of central intelligence, George Tenet, go on repeating the White House formula for a year as well—insisting that it was too soon to reach conclusions, that the Iraq Survey Group was busy in the field and something might still be found? Is it possible that in addition to writing a National Intelligence Estimate which was wrong in every particular, and on top of providing the factual basis for about thirty false or distorted claims of Iraqi weapons activity made in a speech before the United Nations' Security Council by Secretary of State Colin Powell in February 2003—is it possible that in addition to producing these two compendiums of error, the intelligence community really needed a year and a half to conclude that it had been wrong? Think about this for a moment. Before the war, working with the barest smattering of fragmentary information, the CIA could conclude with *high confidence* that these stockpiles existed. But now we are asked to believe that after the war, with unimpeded access to every file, every person, and every street address in Iraq, the CIA could not, over the course of a year, decide whether the stockpiles were there or not?

The obvious answer to this question compels us to register a fact which everyone who pays attention to American intelligence has grown far too accustomed to accepting without comment. By that I mean our reluctance to criticize, or even to note in any audible way, the obvious explanation for Tenet's faithful echoing of the president's tactics of delay. Tenet was protecting the president—not from foreign enemies abroad, but from political opponents at home. Why did Tenet do this? Because he was part of the president's team. What does this tell us about the integrity of American intelligence? What should Congress and the people do about an intelligence service they cannot trust?

In my opinion this is not a minor matter. As long as DCIs defend the president politically, they cannot be trusted to embrace their broader mandate—which is to call them as they see them. And as long as the agency run by the DCI conceals or manipulates information to keep peace with the White House, or goes further and actually marches officials up to Capitol Hill to testify in support of misreadings, distortions, exaggerations, or even outright fabrications, then the agency cannot be trusted either. The close relationship between the White House and the CIA is an old and difficult problem. No president will long tolerate an organization that contradicts him, however quietly and privately. That is a fact of life which DCIs have learned to live with. But at the same time we should not expect Congress or the public to trust or fund an agency indefinitely which allows itself to become a kind of foreign ministry of spin. This is where we find ourselves now—the CIA under George Tenet gradually abandoned its pretense of objectivity and joined the president's claque for war, but Congress has not yet decided how to describe or recognize this fact, or what to do about it.

But severe as the problem already is, it threatens to become still worse as war continues in Iraq and as Porter Goss settles into his position as director of central intelligence, or is perhaps elevated to a newly invented post with more power and broader control over the full community of American intelligence organizations. Goss has arrived in Langley with a history of ever-closer ties to President Bush and his administration. In March 2004 he attacked the Democrats, including John Kerry, for seeking budget cuts which were "devastating to the ability of the CIA to keep America safe." In June he called Kerry "dangerously naive." On arriving at Langley, Goss launched a concerted effort to bottle up contrarian voices inside the CIA. Early efforts to plug leaks led to a major dust-up and the resignations on November 15 of the two highest officials of the agency's clandestine service. Tenet left the agency in July, the same month the National Intelligence Council issued a paper, still classified, which warned of the possibility that Iraq would collapse into civil war. The best-case scenario, the council said, would be a "tenuous stability"; rosier hopes were dropped from the paper as unrealistic.

In September *The New York Times* learned that the NIC had circulated two classified reports in January 2003 warning that the invasion of Iraq would probably divide the country along religious and ethnic lines, bring political violence, and arouse the anger of the Islamic world. President Bush, running for reelection, dismissed the July report as "just guessing," and the longtime CIA analyst in charge of the pessimistic July report, Paul Pillar, was vigorously attacked by *The Wall Street Journal* and the conservative columnist Robert Novak for criticizing administration policy at a private dinner in California.

Also uncomfortably exposed in the spotlight was Michael Scheuer, a counterterror expert who ran the CIA's bin Laden unit for several years in the late 1990s. In the spring of 2004 the agency permitted Scheuer to publish a book criticizing the war on terror, *Imperial Hubris*, but then ordered him to stop discussing it with journalists. Some months back Scheuer sent a letter to the Senate Intelligence Committee citing ten examples of timidity, mismanagement, and dysfunction on the part of intelligence officials who put their careers ahead of their work. When *The Atlantic* published the text of his letter Scheuer resumed giving interviews to journalists, thereby inviting official retaliation. On November 12, Scheuer announced his resignation.

The internal stresses of the CIA, rarely visible to outsiders, are apparent now because the agency has been pressed to test the limits of what long custom has identified as permissible stretching of the evidence to bolster a case or avoid an unwelcome conclusion. In the half-century since it was founded in 1947 analysts have often held views which the White House did not share, and they have consequently learned to endure periods when they are ignored. Carrying the President's Daily Brief to the White House is much like leading a horse to water—the CIA has learned that you can lay your best estimate on the desk in the Oval Office but you can't make a president read it or heed it. The agency makes extraordinary efforts to serve presidents by accommodating their agendas and management styles. Analysts have learned to tackle issues from the end that presidents think important, to be circumspect about conclusions which policymakers resist, to hold back in estimate-drafting sessions when other institutions like the Pentagon take a proprietary interest in some narrow intelligence question, and above all to keep quiet when presidents go their own way. All that is included under the rules of the game as it is played. But the agency in its present form, and the people who staff it, cannot long tolerate a working climate in which they are expected to produce a stream of "intelligence" handcrafted to support an administration's view of the world, or of its progress in the war on terror.

In my view it was a surrender of exactly that sort which explains the National Intelligence Estimate of October 2002, written on the president's behalf to convince Congress that Saddam Hussein represented a threat sufficiently grave and urgent to justify war. How else are we to account for the analysts' failure to get anything right? Debaters might insist that anyone can make a mistake, and everybody else made the same one about Saddam's WMD, but being wrong is not what needs to be explained. The problem is the "high confidence" with which the NIE reached its wrong conclusions, using the barest handful of factual claims which were all arguable and ambiguous.

This is not the place to reargue the claims about the aluminum tubes. We need only consider the process of analysis itself, which measures what could or might be known against what is known. Reporters do this. Historians do this. Criminal prosecutors do this, and they all learn to tell the difference among answers that are spot on, probable, possible, plausible, conceivable, or too thin to utter in public. To accept the Iraqi WMD mistake as honest I would have to believe that CIA analysts steeped in their field of expertise could not tell the difference between a weak case and a strong case. I don't believe that. In my own view they all knew the case was weak but surrendered to pressure from above and hoped to be saved by a miracle —they convinced themselves that *something* would turn up when the troops got to Baghdad and were free to look in all the nooks and crannies. But as Charles Duelfer makes clear in the recently released and exhaustive final report of the CIA's Iraq Survey Group, there was nothing.

Bad as that lapse was, still worse may lie ahead as the administration marches ahead on the course it has chosen. As the war in Iraq unfolds, and perhaps even spreads to neighboring countries, CIA analysts will be expected to address many basic questions about the nature and progress of the struggle. The principal audience for these estimates will of course be in the White House, but the rest of the administration will be watching them as well, and the ancillary consumers of intelligence will be waiting for the telltale public signs that reality and official policy are in harmony, or at war. Both houses of Congress are controlled by Republicans and can be expected to stand by the president—but not forever if success eludes us. How will they know? The bad news always arrives in the same way—as a deepening contradiction between official briefings and what senators and congressmen read over their morning coffee in the pages of *The New York Times* and *The Washington Post*.

The first and most basic question CIA analysts must address in keeping tabs on the progress of the war is whom we are fighting. I do not know of any official answer to this question—just occasional anecdotal answers given by administration officials, starting with the most voluble, Donald Rumsfeld, who has variously described our opponents as die-hard Baathists, dead-enders, and Saddam Hussein loyalists. Also frequently mentioned are forces generally described as "loyal to Abu Musab al-Zarqawi," who is said to be an ally of Osama bin Laden or an associate of al-Qaeda.

The president insists that the war in Iraq is now the central front of the war on terror, and the insurgents' use of car bombs, kidnappings, and beheadings certainly qualifies as terror. But defining our opponents as terrorists disguises the more important fact that most of them, probably in excess of 90 percent, are Iraqis angry at Americans. This should not be hard for us to understand. Americans have invaded their country, have killed anywhere between 10,000 and 100,000 civilians, plus an unknown number of combatants in the regular Iraqi army and the resistance, and have vowed to transform their country politically—beginning with the banishment from public life of scores of thousands of Baath Party members who ran things for thirty years before the Americans came. It's one of the oldest stories in human history—an invasion followed by military occupation backing a client government has encountered resistance. What else would we expect?

But if our reason for war was to counter a threat posed by terrorists with weapons of mass destruction, a threat since proved illusory, while the actual resistance we meet in Iraq is angry and nationalist in an uncomplicated way, then it is hard to escape the conclusion that we are fighting an unnecessary war. This is not a conclusion the White House will want to concede, nor will it be likely to accept the wide circulation of any CIA finding that would support this view. What should we expect instead? My guess would be painstakingly thorough accounts of all foreign elements beginning with al-Zarqawi, much about the prevalence of Islamic extremism within the resistance, and very little about angry Iraqis who hope to drive the Americans away with roadside bombs, or why they might risk their lives to do that. The question of whom we are fighting, awkward now, will become critical if the elections scheduled for January 2005 fail to establish a government Iraqis accept as legitimate. The result of that will be the very thing Rumsfeld derided as preposterous at the outset of the war—a quagmire of the unwinnable sort the United States last experienced in Vietnam, where we spent a decade trying to defend a government that couldn't defend itself.

A second question, closely related, concerns the level of assistance given to the Iraqi resistance by neighboring countries, principally Syria and Iran. Both have been accused by the administration of permitting "terrorists" to cross their borders into Iraq, and Iran has been often warned in addition to abandon its alleged program to build nuclear weapons. The administration's reluctance to recognize the Iraqi resistance as largely homegrown pushes it to exaggerate the role of foreign terrorists, to blame anti-American feeling on meddlers from abroad, to accuse Syria and Iran of sponsoring or harboring terrorists, and to threaten both with regime change as part of a broader strategy of "draining the swamp" of Islamic and terrorist extremism throughout the Middle East. The interim government of Iraq has recently closed the border with Syria and Jordan to halt the influx of foreign fighters, whose motives are too little explored. Do they come to spread "terror," or to drive out the Americans as they once crossed borders to drive the Russians from Afghanistan? CIA estimators will not find it easy to explain why the motive then cannot be the motive now.

But the most difficult question of all for the analysts at the CIA will probably concern the attitudes of foreign governments toward American policy. Tight-lipped skepticism is the best we can expect from the Arabic and Islamic world, where the populace is horrified by the nightly newscasts of civilian casualties, and things do not seem to be going much better among our traditional allies. Of the thirty-two countries which sent troops—in most cases only token units—to join the US in Iraq, fourteen have withdrawn or reduced their forces. Most recent was Hungary, which has announced that it would pull out its three hundred troops before the end of 2004. How will the rest of the coalition, and other traditional allies, respond to threats of still wider war as the United States escalates its pressure on Iran to abandon hope of building nuclear weapons? How will the governments of our traditional allies view such threats—not to mention the governments of Russia and China? What are these governments, some of which are now negotiating with Iran, saying to each other about the war right now?

Edward Creasy, author of *Fifteen Decisive Battles of the World*, published in 1851, writes somewhere that following the Crimean War every discussion in the foreign chanceries of the world soon turned to the question of Russia. The second Bush administration will make it difficult for other countries to treat the war in Iraq as a passing aberration—a "bizarre episode," in the words of Ronald Reagan. Further widening of the war to change regimes in Syria and Iran could open the door to something which the United States has never previously experienced—organized resistance by former friends and allies who oppose American policy and hope to back up their words with practical pressure. This may sound alarmist now, but how many observers expected, much less predicted in public, that the United States would invade and occupy Iraq a year before it happened?

We are on the verge of entering new territory here. I think we should all take careful note of official American remarks about Iran and Syria, but Iran especially; to my ear they closely echo what the administration was saying about Iraq beginning early in 2002—the regime is unelected, it is dominated by extremists, it is embarked on a program to build nuclear weapons, it supports terrorist groups and might give them weapons of mass destruction, the regime is a threat to America. Professional military observers rule out a wider war at the moment for the practical reason that American forces are already stretched to the breaking point. The Pentagon insists there will be no return to the draft, but defense officials also say that the volunteer army works fine, and nothing stands in the way of its expansion but congressional authority and the money to pay troops. Bush ran for reelection as a man who means what he says, and he says he will not tolerate governments that sponsor terror, or the prospect of Iran with a bomb.

Maybe it's only talk this time, but no foreign government will long trust to that. Consider the map. The United States already occupies Afghanistan and Iraq; imagine for a moment that American armies entered Iran as well. Every nation would see immediately that this would constitute a great geopolitical fact—something very much resembling the radical map change feared by the Carter administration in 1979 when the Soviet Union invaded Afghanistan and the Shah of Iran was overthrown by a radical fundamentalist cleric. Twenty-five years ago it was not the Americans alone who feared that one more step would put Russian armies on the shore of the Persian Gulf after a century of trying. Only a dozen years ago, when Saddam Hussein invaded and occupied Kuwait, the whole world joined a grand coalition led by the United States to evict him. Would the governments of France, Germany, Russia, and China, trusting to American good intentions, take a more relaxed view of long-term American military domination of the oil-producing states of the Middle East? I'm guessing not, and once joined such a conflict might last fifty years.

But in this world guessing is not good enough. To make our way safely through this quagmire we would need to know how foreign governments felt about our plans, and what, if anything, they planned to do in response. The president would need to know, of course, but so would Congress and the people before contemplating, permitting, or agreeing to pay for a step so momentous. My purpose is not to nail down the probability of a wider war; it is only to suggest that the American intelligence universe is already shifting in profound ways. Not long ago it was a simple matter for American governments to learn how the French and the Germans felt about something; all they had to do was ask. With matters as they stand now I'm not so sure. But I suspect that the suspicion and cross-purposes dividing us from old allies have already carried us into a new realm, and it would not surprise me to read tomorrow or the next day that some American agricultural attaché in Paris or Berlin was being expelled for activities incompatible with his post.

The toughest challenge for anyone trying to pay attention to the world is to grasp the large shape of events—not the details of warming or cooling relations as routine issues come and go, but the sea change when everything begins to shift. In the world at the moment the big unknown is what America is up to. Following Bush's reelection we must expect the question of American intentions to enter the discussion in the foreign chanceries of the entire world. These intentions are not transparent. The administration first argued that it sought only to disarm Saddam. When that turned out to be unnecessary it was ready with a new argument—replacing Saddam with a free, democratic government would create a beacon of hope and a light unto the nations, persuading terrorists to give up the struggle and changing the political landscape of the Middle East.

Maybe that was the real reason all along, and maybe not. Foreign governments may feel that a better guide would be the president's national security strategy issued in late 2001. There the administration argued for a policy of preemption, and a forward policy projecting American military power into the heart of the Middle East. A forward policy requires client states on the ground. What sort of client states? How big a military presence? To remain how long? Those are the kind of questions foreign chanceries will want to answer.

A parallel question for us is what is happening to American intelligence as the president's policy is gradually revealed. The CIA's operations and reading of events have always been pregnant with political significance but over the last four years we have seen the beginning of what I would describe as a sea change—from an agency uneasily aware of the possible political impact of everything it does and says, because presidents never let them forget it, to an agency turning by slow degrees into an operational arm of the White House, not only doing or attempting to do what presidents ask, but one increasingly willing to play a team role, to describe the world as the president sees it, and to lend its authority to "intelligence" the president can use to carry along Congress and the public.

We must not pretend to be surprised at this. We have just watched it happen. Fear of Saddam Hussein's illusory weapons of mass destruction was used by the president to frighten and intimidate Congress into voting for war. Kindness permits us to call this an honest mistake once, but only once. Next time we will have to conclude that the CIA can no longer be trusted, and matters will deteriorate from there.

—*The New York Review of Books*, December 16, 2004

5

BLACK ARTS

"CHATTER" SEEMS TOO CASUAL A WORD for what is arguably the most important single product of the mammoth American cyber-industrial establishment which gathers "communications intelligence," commonly abbreviated as Comint. Intelligence professionals use "chatter" to describe the miscellany they acquire of the personal and operational communications of "persons of interest," another term of art meaning people who may know or be planning something the United States wants or needs to know about. Since 2001 the people at the top of the American list of persons of interest have included Osama bin Laden, his lieutenants, associates, and supporters in al-Qaeda, and the widening circles of Islamic fundamentalists who share or know or have heard rumors about Osama's goals and plans. In the absence of agents reporting from al-Qaeda's innermost sanctum, American intelligence professionals must depend on chatter to keep track of whatever devastating attacks al-Qaeda's terrorist cells may be planning next.

Over the spring and summer of 2001 intercepts of terrorist chatter rose to dramatic levels but were shrugged off by the White House and the president's then national security adviser, Condoleezza Rice. The destruction of the World Trade Center ended that; now the nation's electronic ears strain for every terrorist whisper. Periodic official warnings of new attacks on tunnels and bridges, on major sports events, on commercial airliners arriving from France, and on the New York City subway system have all been identified as prompted by chatter, often described as reaching levels not seen since just before September 11—shorthand for "listen up, this is serious." In the case of New York's subways some 16,000 law enforcement personnel in and out of uniform were mobilized after Comint analysts lifted a single worrying word from the chatter—"underground." What did it mean? No one knew, but responsible officials were not about to wait and see.

But what is chatter exactly? As an American graduate student in Britain in the late 1990s Patrick Keefe came to the subject through news stories about "Echelon"—the code name, first published in 1988, for a coordinated, decades-long global effort by English-speaking countries to intercept communications of intelligence interest. The reluctance of governments to explain what they were doing and why encouraged periodic waves of popular fear that around the corner loomed the omnipresent Big Brother of George Orwell's novel *1984*. These alarms were given semi-official voice in 1998 after a committee of the European Parliament, concerned that Echelon was aimed at them, commissioned a social scientist to write "An Appraisal of the Technologies of Political Control." The report's author stated flatly that the eavesdroppers did not just have the technology to listen in; they used it:

> Within Europe, all email, telephone and fax communications are routinely intercepted by the United States National Security Agency, transferring all target information from the European mainland via the Strategic hub of London then by Satellite to Fort Meade in Maryland via the crucial hub at Menwith Hill in the North York Moors of the UK.

That word "all" was intended to attract attention and it did. The cold war had been over for a decade, and terrorism had not yet replaced the Red Army as a threat; what were the listeners listening to?

Keefe began his investigation in the pre–September 11 days, before al-Qaeda proved that mega-terrorism was not an idle threat. Things look very different now when it is widely believed that a few more listeners, quicker off the mark, might have prevented the catastrophic attack that brought down the World Trade Center. Just how close American intelligence came to acting in time, and the deeply rooted reasons it did not, can be found in *Blind Spot*, Timothy Naftali's useful new history of the American education in counterterrorism since the Second World War.[1]

That education began with overexcited (and unfounded) fears of a die-hard Nazi terror campaign in the last days of the war, then adapted to the back-alley violence of the early days of the cold war, when the United States and its allies supported resistance groups in the Ukraine and the Baltic countries, and the KGB's Department 13 responded with attempts, some successful, to assassinate anti-Communist activists plotting against the Soviets.

But it was not until the Six-Day War in 1967 that Americans really began to grasp the challenge of terrorism. In the wake of Israel's whirlwind victory, Palestinians fought back with terror, the traditional weapon of the weak, and the early cross-border attacks on Israel, rarely successful, were soon followed by attacks in a larger arena harder to defend—pretty much the whole of Europe. Bloody assaults of the sort that targeted travelers lined up at ticket counters never achieved much, but some governments, like the mullahs' Iran and Qaddhafi's Libya, grew confident over time that they could attack America and its allies at will with little fear of retaliation.

---

1. *Blind Spot: The Secret History of American Counterterrorism* (Basic Books, 2005).

Naftali is a scholar of national security issues who has specialized in secret intelligence, and *Blind Spot* is built on long familiarity with the secret organizations responsible for the "counter" in counterterrorism. Few Americans will recall much beyond the names of once-feared terrorists like Abu Nidal and Carlos ("the Jackal") for the good reason that both were driven from the field by an aggressive CIA-supported campaign to cut off their funds, arrest or kill their operatives, and warn their government sponsors to stand down or accept the consequences. But paradoxically, Naftali argues, those successes did not take. Vigorous counterterror efforts were followed by growing White House timidity, which contributed to the now much-discussed risk-averse culture of the CIA.

The ordeal of the Iran-contra scandal was partly to blame for driving counterterror efforts into reverse, and the rest, Naftali writes, can be blamed on "bureaucratic languor"—his phrase for the go-slow, think-twice institutional caution which follows when presidents lose their stomach for the hard decisions required to fight dirty wars. Naftali does not make the argument that getting tough is all it will take to win the war on terror, but he points firmly to a fatal White House omission during the two or three years before September 11—recognition that al-Qaeda was capable, determined, and dangerous.

But the new American determination in the war on terror does not provide a kind of blank-check justification of whatever it is that intelligence organizations might like to do. The Echelon which caught Patrick Keefe's interest in the late 1990s may have added some Arabic-language speakers to its staff, and the mood at various communications intelligence headquarters may have a new urgency, but Echelon itself remains the same. Official explanations of what that urgency may involve do not proceed from the general to the specific. The phrase "matters of intelligence interest" is about as concrete as any announcement gets. Wanting more, Keefe set out to answer this question for himself, and his book, *Chatter: Dispatches from the Secret*

World of Global Eavesdropping,[2] recounts his travels and conversations with many people worried about government intrusion and a few people with actual experience of the Comint world.

The result is a kind of naturalist's ramble around the fenced perimeter of the whole vast establishment of technical gear used for intercepting communications. Some things become abundantly clear. For example, it's called "global eavesdropping" because listening posts circle the globe. The big Echelon stations, Keefe tells us, are Morwenstow in Britain, Sugar Grove in West Virginia, and the Yakima Training Center in Washington State. Secondary stations come and go with changing politics and borders; once-important listening posts in northern Iran, Hong Kong, and southern Germany have been abandoned, while others have been cranked up to take their place.

Some of these date back to the earliest days of British–American cooperation in collecting Comint, like the nine-hundred-person Composite Signals Organization based on Ascension Island in the South Atlantic, where green sea turtles are welcomed on their annual migration from the coast of Brazil but no one else may step ashore without official clearance. The rules are the same on Diego Garcia in the Indian Ocean, retained as a territory by Britain when it granted independence to the Seychelles and Mauritius in the 1960s. To simplify the secret-keeping, the British simply removed Diego Garcia's two thousand people to Mauritius, where they soon began to pine for home. After decades of supplication a visit was planned for November 2001, but the war on terror intervened. The island is now too busy as a listening post and air force base to tolerate visitors who were, in point of fact, born there.

Chatter contains a lot of information of this sort—names of bases and organizations, descriptions of technologies used for collecting information, a sketchy outline history of the Anglophone alliance

---

2. Random House, 2005.

beginning in 1946 with the original British and American agreement. Over time Canada, New Zealand, and Australia joined the club but the Americans remain dominant, putting up the money and doling out the take. Other countries maintain listening programs of their own but none can match the American reach, a fact that worries Europeans. In the course of his travels Keefe met just about everybody trying to penetrate the secrets of Echelon and gradually he learned what it is—up to a point.

His education began with the remark of a former British intelligence officer, Alistair Harley, who told him that "if it uses radio waves then [it can] be intercepted, monitored, stored." The "it" here means people trying to communicate, and radio waves are used to convey just about everything that isn't written down on hand-delivered paper or transmitted over secure landlines. The most important single fact about Comint is that there is a lot of it, roughly all the daily communications of the politically or commercially active part of the human race, both written and spoken. How much talk are we talking about? Well, it certainly exceeds the conversations (if we could overhear and record them) of everybody in a baseball stadium during a World Series game, plus the conversations of everybody watching it on television, plus the remarks that all the watchers combined have made or heard over the last...week? year? decade? There is a lot of talk going on, and all the talkers are talking at once. The problem is to separate the words of urgent interest from the roar of background chatter. This is where Echelon comes in.

"Echelon," Keefe learned, "is nothing more than a secret code name for a specific computer program used to sort through intercepted satellite communications." Lest reference to satellite communications be interpreted as bringing the problem down to size, Keefe reminds us that over the course of the 1990s the number of cell phones in use increased from 16 million to 741 million, the number of Internet users increased from 4 million to 361 million, and the annual number of minutes devoted to international telephone conversations increased from 38 billion to 100 billion. At one point or another almost all of that talk passes from the surface of the earth to a satellite and back again—the moment when the eavesdroppers pick it up. But the sorting job is beyond human eavesdroppers; half the population would be required to listen to the other half. "Echelon," Keefe writes in a second pass at definition, "refers to a particular type of computer that is used to sort through large amounts of data for items on a given watch list." Keefe has not learned much about exactly how this is done, but even that little is helpful in providing a sense of the magnitude of the challenge.

The work, Keefe explains, begins with establishing two lists—one of persons and organizations (the "watch list"), and a second of "keywords" that make the intelligence ear perk up. These lists are collected in "Echelon Dictionaries," which are maintained by dictionary managers responsible for putting names and words in or taking them out. Osama would be on the watch list, and "bomb" and "attack" and "anthrax" and "New York City's water supply" would be among the keywords, along with many others. Finding them in the ocean of chatter begins with "packet sniffers," which check the "data packets" that transmit communications in electronic form. When the sniffer finds a match between address or message and watch list or keyword, it copies the message for further examination—the moment at which human beings begin to be involved.

Here written communications present one kind of a problem and voice communications another, generally considered more difficult. To sort out the second type requires a "word-spotting" capacity— essentially a computer program that can distinguish between spoken words in a multitude of languages and is not fooled by synonyms— "device" for bomb, say, or "sniffles" for smallpox. Admiral Bobby Ray Inman, a longtime director of the American codebreaking and Comint efforts as chief of the NSA, once admitted in public that word spotting for voice systems remained a dream. "I have wasted more US taxpayers' dollars trying to do that," he said, "than [on] anything else in my intelligence career."

Classic chatter is the target of these global Comint search efforts, and while everything is within reach, it is hard to spot the significant in time to make use of it. On September 10, 2001, Keefe reminds us, two messages in Arabic were intercepted in the course of transmission from Afghanistan to Saudi Arabia. Both rang the al-Qaeda bell and were retrieved for translation and analysis. When they were read two days later one said, "Tomorrow is zero hour," and the other, "The match begins tomorrow." Would translation of those two messages in good time have served as the two-by-four once used by sharecropping farmers to catch the attention of balky mules? No one really thinks so, although vast sums have been recommended and will doubtless be spent to speed up the entire effort to sift terrorist chatter for timely warning of the next attack.

After years of studying this problem, Keefe, like the European Parliament, concludes that Echelon is not intended as Big Brother's foot in the door, but represents a good-faith effort to solve a genuine problem with state-of-the-art computers and programs which (it is hoped) might succeed in penetrating terrorist cells where traditional spies have been dismissed as bound to fail. The secrecy that envelops Echelon is not sinister but practical; when people don't know what you're doing they can't stop you, and they can't protect against it.

But chatter is not the only target of the NSA; the listeners also target individuals, groups, and places to monitor conversations that might give the United States secret advantage in the effort to do what it wants to do. The most interesting section of Keefe's book retells the story, only sketchily reported in *The New York Times* and *The Washington Post* as it unfolded, of the joint British and American effort to monitor the communications of UN Secretary General Kofi Annan and the diplomatic traffic of Security Council members as they sought guidance early in 2003 from their home governments for dealing with the relentless American effort to browbeat the council into voting for war on Iraq.

The episode surfaced in public in a manner of utmost rarity—a deliberate leak to the press by a career employee of an intelligence organization, in this case a translator for Britain's Government Communications Headquarters (GCHQ) in Cheltenham. After four days of agonized indecision the translator, Katharine Gunn, gave a document to a friend with connections in the mass media. A month later it appeared on the front page of *The Observer*, giving the world a raw glimpse into the boiler-room reality of communications intelligence. The document was a January 31 memo to GCHQ from Frank Koza, chief of staff for regional targets of the American National Security Agency. Koza wrote to his GCHQ colleagues:

> As you've likely heard by now, the Agency is mounting a surge particularly directed at the UN Security Council (UNSC) members (minus US and GBR of course) for insights as to how to [*sic*] membership is reacting to the ongoing debate RE: Iraq... the whole gamut of information that could give US policymakers an edge in obtaining results favorable to US goals or to head off surprises.

The surge being mounted was in efforts to bug conversations and intercept communications among UN delegates as part of the American strong-arm effort to get a favorable Security Council vote, but by the time Koza's memo was published the debate was over and the US was on the verge of going to war. An internal investigation was immediately launched by GCHQ and after a day of denial Gunn told her boss, "The leak was me."[3] A year of cat and mouse followed before

---

3. See Patrick Radden Keefe, "The Leak Was Me," *The New York Review of Books*, June 10, 2004.

the British authorities decided not to prosecute the case, but when Keefe finally arranged an interview with the twenty-eight-year-old Gunn he found that she still was not free to answer even the simplest questions about Echelon:

> "But it's a name you've heard before?" I pushed.
> "Yes," Katharine said slowly, looking me in the eyes. "But I can't comment on that either."

The only remarkable thing about the Koza memo is that it got published. In every other way it appears to have been a routine exchange between the NSA and GCHQ of the sort that has occurred daily for fifty years. *Chatter* is the latest in a series of books to explain what Comint is and does, and while it is written with fluid grace and disciplined structure, in truth it does not add much hard new information to what has already been published by the two acknowledged masters of the field—David Kahn, whose history *The Codebreakers* remains the standard text nearly forty years after it was first published, and James Bamford, whose two books on the NSA have revealed pretty much all the public knows about the black cube in the Maryland countryside once called "No Such Agency."[4]

Over the years there have been occasional moments of aroused public scrutiny when intelligence collection is suddenly glimpsed at work—for example, when an American ELINT plane was shot down after ignoring Chinese warnings to back off, or when the CIA's then chief William Casey threatened to arrest the *Washington Post* reporter Bob Woodward for spilling the beans about a US program to tap Soviet

---

4. David Kahn, *The Codebreakers: The Story of Secret Writing* (Macmillan, 1967); James Bamford, *The Puzzle Palace: A Report of America's Most Secret Agency* (Houghton Mifflin, 1982) and *Body of Secrets: Anatomy of the Ultra-secret National Security Agency from the Cold War Through the Dawn of a New Century* (Doubleday, 2001).

underseas telephone cables, or when the reporter Seymour Hersh revealed that CIA operatives had been routinely opening first-class mail sent to or by US citizens on a watch list of antiwar activists, or when the US pushed a boatload of NSA eavesdroppers so close to the scene of fighting during the Six-Day War that Israeli planes sank the craft with the loss of thirty-seven American lives. But with those exceptions and a few others, all forgotten with amazing rapidity, the public record is empty of any kind of sustained discussion of what Comint is for or costs, where it succeeds or fails, what it collects, who gets to read it, and who decides. About all the public really knows is that the NSA is *big*.

It wasn't always big. In the spring of 1919, when the father of American cryptography, Herbert O. Yardley, drew up a plan for a permanent State Department codebreaking organization—a "black chamber," in traditional European parlance—he estimated that a modest $100,000 a year would buy a chief (Yardley) and fifty clerks and cryptanalysts. In the event the staff was half that and the budget for the new organization was split by State and the Army, which wanted a hand in. Yardley rented a three-story building in New York City, a choice mandated by federal law, which prohibited the State Department from adding new employees to its staff in Washington. There, on East 38th Street just off Fifth Avenue, Yardley put two dozen people to work under civilian cover—as the Code Compiling Company, incorporated in New York to produce and sell commercial codes. Thus concealed, Yardley's shop was to collect and decipher foreign communications of interest to American diplomats and soldiers.

The first challenge was to get copies of cables, in theory protected by law from release to unauthorized persons. Yardley got around this easily enough by simply asking cable companies to hand them over. What he told them is unknown, but it worked. The head of the American Cable Company told him, "The government can have anything it wants," and other firms were also obliging in varying degree. By the end of its first year the Cipher Bureau, as it was formally known, was solving and reading a multitude of foreign codes.

Yardley is one of the remarkable men in American history. He is known primarily for his summary dismissal in 1929 by incoming Secretary of State Henry Stimson, a patrician Wall Street lawyer who closed down the Cipher Bureau with the casual observation that "gentlemen do not read each other's mail"—a remark, interestingly, which is the only thing remembered about either man. It is often cited as marking the high-water mark of American starched-collar idealism before the downhill slide into great-power realism. But what made Yardley famous is not the thing that makes him interesting. The son of a railroad telegrapher, a man with a lively Jazz Age interest in money, good-looking women, and drinks at five, Yardley not only taught his country how to read other people's mail but wrote two of the enduring American books—the best single intelligence memoir, *The American Black Chamber* (1931), and perhaps the greatest book in any language on playing cards for money, *The Education of a Poker Player* (1957).

Either might have justified a biography long since but two barriers intervened. One was the enduring anger aroused among officials by Yardley's cool account in the first of his great books of the routine deceptions of government when no one is watching. Fair judges might have noted that Yardley was out of a job and needed the money when he wrote *The American Black Chamber*, and that the government had announced in effect that it was getting out of the codebreaking business for good, leaving Yardley's revelations interesting but moot. Such excuses cut no ice; in the three decades that Yardley survived the Cipher Bureau, official anger never relented a degree. Time and again Yardley was blocked, ignored, blacklisted, or secretly undermined— an eloquent demonstration of what intelligence professionals and their employers do to those who break the code. Laws against speaking out of school are hardly necessary; the freeze-out is enough.

But Yardley remains the great figure of American codebreaking and it was probably inevitable that David Kahn, the great historian of American codebreaking, would set out to write his biography. From the outset he was challenged by the second major barrier to writing Yardley's life—lack of materials. When Yardley speaks in his books—there is a third covering his adventures in China in the 1930s—all is illuminated, but where the books stop the life grows dim. At his death, Yardley left no papers—odd for a writer—but when intelligence figures die it is not uncommon for personable men to arrive promptly at the widow's door with an offer to help. Typically the visit ends with every scrap of paper going out the door before the sun goes down. Kahn offers no guess about the fate of Yardley's missing papers, and repaired the deficiency in the only way—by scouring every plausible archive, talking to the bare handful of survivors, and trusting to luck. His big finds were the files of Yardley's literary agent, George Bye, preserved in the library of Columbia University, and the letters Yardley sent home from China during the year and a half he worked for the legendary chief of Kuomintang intelligence, Dai Li.

The man who emerges in Kahn's briskly paced portrait[5] is gifted, complex, resourceful, and often disappointed. Yardley's life included more periods of drinking than not, some interesting women, and many spurned efforts to resume the work he knew and liked best. He bounced back from the loss of his codebreaking job with *The American Black Chamber*, hung around Hollywood long enough to earn $10,000 for doing nothing, wrote some forgettable novels, did some radio work, dabbled in real estate, and finally got back into the great game, attacking Japanese codes for officials in China. During after-hours in the Chungking Hostel he taught the young reporter Theodore

---

5. *The Reader of Gentlemen's Mail: Herbert O. Yardley and the Birth of American Code-breaking* (Yale University Press, 2004).

White two useful survival arts—how to play poker and how to ride out an air raid, later summarized by White in a memoir:

> The chief danger of an air raid, he said, was splintered glass from windows. Thus, when one hears the siren one should get a drink, lie down on a couch and put two pillows over oneself— one pillow over the eyes and the other over the groin... if the eyes or groin were injured, life was not worth living. It was good advice for any groundling in the age before atom bombs; and I took it.

After leaving China in mid-1940 Yardley briefly worked for Canadian intelligence, but a few sharp words from Washington ended the job and seemed to take the fight out of him. Back home he was employed by the Office of Price Administration for the last half of World War II, then moved sideways in 1947 to become a public housing bureaucrat. He died in 1958.

We might study Yardley's life with profit for the poker, but Kahn of course gives pride of place to the making and breaking of codes, and there are wonderful accounts in *The Reader of Gentlemen's Mail* of some of Yardley's greatest feats. Here Kahn's mastery of the field gives his book genuine intellectual excitement; solving a code involves a kind of personal combat like chess, with the added drama that the loser generally does not learn of his defeat until it is too late.

Kahn is frank to admit that Yardley was not the greatest American codebreaker; his chief rival, William Friedman, was a duller man, but he broke many wartime Japanese codes, was smarter than Yardley, did more to advance the art, and solved wartime messages that made a bigger difference to the course of history. But Yardley was first on the scene, he left an account of the secret world which is unsurpassed, and on one notable occasion his solution of a code allowed US diplomats to sit tight in a down-to-the wire negotiation limiting Japan's navy because they had read the official instructions telling Japan when to give in.

The scene was Washington, November and December 1921. The world's naval powers had come to negotiate limits to shipbuilding to prevent a runaway naval race and save money. The point in contention was the ratio of tonnage afloat between the three largest navies, those of Britain, the United States, and Japan. The US proposed a ratio of 10:10:6—limiting the British and Americans to 500,000 gross tons of naval shipping, and the Japanese to 300,000 tons. But the Japanese were unhappy and would not budge from their insistence on a 10:10:7 ratio, which would give them 350,000 tons. As Kahn makes clear this was not a distinction without a difference. Calculations difficult to summarize here meant that Western navies would be at a disadvantage in Japanese waters with a 10:10:7 ratio, but would have ships enough to dominate even far from home ports if they could insist successfully on 10:10:6. It was at this moment that Yardley earned his place in history.

Two years earlier after months of work Yardley had solved an important Japanese diplomatic code; a later variant was broken in the summer of 1921, and on December 2, as the naval conference struggled over its impasse on the ratio, a copy of a cable from Tokyo was delivered to Yardley's team and deciphered almost as quickly as a clerk could type. The drift of the message, contained in sixty-three ten-letter groups, was an instruction to Japan's negotiators to defend the ratio tenaciously, falling back one by one through the four positions only as required to prevent the negotiations from breaking down entirely. As Yardley later described in *The American Black Chamber*, infuriating official Washington, position number four was agreement to the 10:10:6 ratio. "Stud poker," Yardley wrote, "is not a very difficult game after you see your opponent's hole card." So it proved. On December 12 the Japanese caved. Set aside all the other solutions achieved by the Cipher Bureau during its ten-year life for a total expenditure of only a third of a million dollars; "this alone," Kahn writes, "made it worth the money spent on it."

But as so often in life and in the intelligence business, things were not entirely as they seemed. Yardley was not the only one trying to read Japanese intentions. A new Japanese ruler, Crown Prince Hirohito, had just taken power in Japan. On November 28, four days before Yardley even saw the critical cable to Japan's chief negotiator, *The New York Times* reported that "Tokyo Is Prepared to Yield on Ratio." Two days later it told readers that the crisis had passed and agreement on the stricter ratio was likely in a week's time. How did the *Times* achieve this feat of prediction while Yardley's Cipher Bureau was still decoding old messages telling the negotiators to stand fast? The short answer appears to be reporting; they stuck close to the Japanese negotiators, and when the wind began to change, one of them told the *Times* what to expect.

Kahn is of two minds about this turn of events. As a lover of neatly wrought code solutions he is full of admiration for what Yardley did and the confidence it gave American diplomats to wait patiently for the apple to fall in Washington's lap. Codebreaking, he writes at the end of the book, "alone provides believable, high-level, unmediated, voluminous, continuous, cheap information." True enough, when the analysts find the solution and find it in time. But as a realist Kahn also admits that there was something anticlimactic about Yardley's greatest achievement. He helped his country win a hand in high-stakes international poker, and was rewarded for his feat with a special commendation and a bonus of $184, but his solution changed nothing: that hand was going to the Americans anyway.

Has the globe-encircling NSA done better than Yardley's tiny bucket shop on East 38th Street? Have the billions spent on satellite collection systems and computer programs like Echelon delivered value for money? Have they made America safer? Intelligence professionals whisper about seldom-touted successes and Patrick Keefe concedes in effect that even a blind hog will find the occasional acorn. But his final judgment is harsh: "Chatter is, as it turns out, a perfect word for the conversations culled from the airwaves: fickle, misleading, most often inconsequential." September 11 was the test. No matter how success is defined by the intelligence world, the Anglophone countries and their listening posts fell short. Comint, Keefe states bluntly, "had its day and failed."

About the failure everyone now agrees. But what was the problem? And what should be done to make us safe? Keefe has no idea. Sounding a little dispirited after his years of research and writing, he urges Americans to think hard about where to draw the line between liberty and security, but it's an odd note on which to conclude. It wasn't respect for the Constitution that kept the NSA from reading the "Tomorrow is zero hour" message until the day after the disaster. It was lack of translators. To meet that kind of problem, the Comint professionals have a default solution: more. Not just more Arab linguists but more of everything—more analysts, more polygraph examiners and security guards, more freedom to listen in on more people, more listening posts, more coverage, more secrecy. Is more what we really need? In my opinion not. Ordinary reporters scooped Yardley in 1921, and ordinary spies—human agents, run by case officers in the field—are most likely to penetrate the heart of terrorist circles now. But running spies is not the NSA's job. Listening is, and more listening is what the NSA knows how to organize, more is what Congress is ready to support and fund, more is what the president wants, and more is what we are going to get.

—*The New York Review of Books*, May 12, 2005

6

BRINGING 'EM ON

IN THE REAL WORLD—and the United States exists in the real world, despite a national weakness for wishful thinking—failure has consequences. The prospects for American success in Iraq, which do not look promising, are the consequence of a cascading series of previous failures—the failure to heed intelligence warnings before September 11, the failure to focus on Osama bin Laden until he was caught, the failure to think twice before invading Iraq, the failure to send enough troops to establish security once the Iraqi army quit fighting, the failure to recognize the growing insurgency until it was too big to crush, the failure to begin building an Iraqi army and police services in a timely manner, the failure to forsee that a war in Iraq would draw jihadists from every corner of the Islamic world....

These failures are all the doing of President Bush and the remarkably small group of intimate advisers who have been running the American government since the state of Florida quit trying to count votes in the 2000 presidential election. Confident at every turn that they knew what to do, impatient of contrary views, strengthened by Republican control of both houses of Congress, and deliberating in a degree of secrecy which the old Soviet Politburo might have envied, President Bush and his team have probably pursued their chosen course with a freer reign and less resistance than any other administration in

American history. Naturally they do not concede failure. The White House argues that the story isn't over yet, Iraq is on the way to becoming a functioning democracy, the insurgency will wither as Sunnis embrace electoral politics, and success of the whole project is still possible if we don't cut and run. Who does not hope the administration is right? Or worry that the tidal pull of events is all in a different direction—toward civil war and spreading violence?

Making sense of this slow spiral of deepening trouble is bound to occupy analysts and historians for a generation to come; weaving through it they will doubtless find some mix of the national attributes that allowed a previous president and his confident advisers to march the country wide-eyed into Vietnam. The challenge in both cases was to create a friendly regime strong enough to let Americans leave, the subject of two recent magazine articles—"Iraq: Learning the Lessons of Vietnam"[1] by Melvin Laird, President Nixon's secretary of defense, who argues that he had the circle squared until Congress cut off funding for South Vietnam; and "Why Iraq Has No Army"[2] by James Fallows, who worries that the administration is whistling Dixie while American popular support for the war drains away and efforts to build Iraqi security forces are allowed to slide. Fallows quotes a Marine lieutenant colonel who thinks the difference between failure in Vietnam and failure now would be a continuing threat from a Sunni remnant of Iraq with a burning jihadist hate for the United States. "In Vietnam we just lost," he told Fallows. "This would be losing with consequences."

The consequence foreseen by Daniel Benjamin and Steven Simon, experts on terrorism and former members of the National Security Council under President Clinton, is implicit in the title of their book *The Next Attack: The Failure of the War on Terror and a Strategy for*

---

1. *Foreign Affairs*, November/December 2005.

2. The Atlantic, December 2005.

Getting it Right.[3] A long chapter examines the familiar list of awful possibilities for painful blows inflicted on the United States by terrorists simply taking advantage of loopholes in our domestic defenses. Some nine million shipping containers bring freight into the United States every year, Benjamin and Simon note; only one in twenty is inspected and any one of the other nineteen could contain explosives, biological agents, fissionable material, even a working atomic bomb. Or a well-placed bomb in a huge industrial plant producing toxic chemicals or dangerous gases might generate an "American Bhopal." Occasionally their worrries verge on fretting; what are terrorists going to do with ultralight aircraft, which strain to get one man aloft with a water bottle?

Benjamin and Simon make a strong case that the president's friend Tom Ridge did a poor job of getting the Department of Homeland Security up and running, and they snap the ruler sharply on the backs of the hands of the women President Bush chose to press the American case in the Islamic world through "public diplomacy"—Charlotte Beers, Margaret Tutwiler, and Karen Hughes, who all managed to achieve little while looking silly. But the "next attack," painful as it may prove to be, is not really the central concern of Benjamin and Simon. Their previous book, *The Age of Sacred Terror: Radical Islam's War Against America,*[4] mapped out their chosen territory, which is the fundamentalist rejection of Western values throughout the Muslim world. What animates them now is the new dangers and troubling turns which have followed the invasion of Iraq, which they identify as "America's first war of choice"—the spreading animosity toward the United States among onetime allies, the spread of jihadism in the Muslim diaspora in the West, the ready access to terrorist technology on the Internet, and the second wave of devastating attacks in

---

3. Times Books, 2005.

4. Random House, 2002.

Spain and Britain by "self-starters" who seem to arrive from nowhere, making it all but impossible to predict succeeding blows.

The United States, they argue, has its hands full trying to stem the growing insurgency in Iraq; how will the administration handle challenges elsewhere in the Islamic world? They quote an intelligence official who described Saudi Arabia, home of the great majority of September 11 hijackers and suicide bombers in Iraq alike, as "the aircraft carrier of the jihad." Pakistan they identify as "the most anti-American country in the world," using the words of the scholar Stephen Cohen. Opinion polls show a Pakistani approval rating of 65 percent for Osama bin Laden, who has probably been hiding in the tribal areas along Pakistan's border with Afghanistan since an over-confident US military allowed him to slip away from Tora Bora. The president of Pakistan, Pervez Musharraf, has narrowly escaped numerous assassination attempts; a successful one could throw control of the country, and of its nuclear weapons, into the hands of Islamic extremists. From Chechnya to Indonesia Benjamin and Simon track a seething hatred of America, fed by images of the war in Iraq, which President Bush and Vice President Cheney habitually call "the central front in the war on terror." Better Baghdad than Boston, is the idea. When insurgent bombs first started to kill American soldiers in the summer of 2003, President Bush seemed unfazed. "Bring 'em on," he said.

For Benjamin and Simon "getting it right" means all the obvious things—putting terrorists out of business, controlling dangerous technologies, protecting the targets that matter most, and trying to open some kind of dialogue with the Islamic world. But the best tool for doing these things is not the US Army. "The Bush administration," they write, "has seriously over-militarized the effort to stop jihadist terror." Doing better, in their view, means dropping the President's strategy of using the military to kill all the terrorists—a futile approach, as would have been apparent to anyone who had actually served in Vietnam, or wondered why the endlessly growing body count was followed by defeat.

But calling the invasion of Iraq "misguided" does not really explain what has gone wrong, and doing better on a national security punch-list is not really a strategy for turning things around. The magnitude of the problem is suggested by the fact that two writers with as much experience as Benjamin and Simon at this point don't really know what to do next. But their book still takes an important first step in the direction of realism by arguing in sober detail that the bright hopes and confident ideas behind the invasion of Iraq were illusions. Nothing dies harder, as Vietnam taught us, and it will take another year or two for that fact to really sink in on a national scale. But in my view it will, and then the hard part can begin.

—*The New York Times Book Review*, December 25, 2005

7

'THE BIGGEST SECRET'

THE CHALLENGES POSED TO AMERICAN DEMOCRACY by secrecy and by unchecked presidential power are the two great themes running through the history of the Iraq war. How long the war will last, who will "win," and what it will do to the political landscape of the Middle East will not be obvious for years to come, but the answers to those questions cannot alter the character of what happened at the outset. Put plainly, the president decided to attack Iraq, he brushed caution and objection aside, and Congress, the press, and the people, with very few exceptions, stepped back out of the way and let him do it.

Explaining this fact is not going to be easy. Commentators often now refer to President Bush's decision to invade Iraq as "a war of choice," which means that it was not provoked. The usual word for an unprovoked attack is aggression. Why did Americans—elected representatives and plain citizens alike—accede so readily to this act of aggression, and why did they question the president's arguments for war so feebly? The whole business is painfully awkward to consider, but it will not go away. If the Constitution forbids a president anything it forbids war on his say-so, and if it insists on anything it insists that presidents are not above the law. In plain terms this means that presidents cannot enact laws on their own, or ignore laws that have been enacted by Congress.

The Foreign Intelligence Surveillance Act (FISA) of 1978 is such a law; it was enacted to end years of routine wiretapping of American citizens who had attracted official attention by opposing the war in Vietnam. The express purpose of the act was to limit what presidents could ask intelligence organizations to do. But for limits on presidential power to have meaning Congress and the courts must have the fortitude to say no when they think no is the answer.

In public life as in kindergarten, the all-important word is no. We are living with the consequences of the inability to say no to the president's war of choice with Iraq, and we shall soon see how Congress and the courts will respond to the latest challenge from the White House—the claim by President Bush that he has the right to ignore FISA's prohibition of government intrusion on the private communications of Americans without a court order, and his repeated statements that he intends to go right on doing it.

Nobody was supposed to know that FISA had been brushed aside. The fact that the National Security Agency (NSA), America's largest intelligence organization, had been turned loose to intercept the faxes, e-mails, and phone conversations of Americans with blanket permission by the president remained secret until the *New York Times* reporters James Risen and Eric Lichtblau learned in 2004 that it was happening. An early version of the story was apparently submitted to the *Times*'s editors in October 2004, when it might have affected the outcome of the presidential election. But the *Times*, for reasons it has not clearly explained, withheld the story until mid-December, when the newspaper's publisher and executive editor—Arthur Sulzberger Jr. and Bill Keller—met with President Bush in the Oval Office to hear his objections before going ahead. Even then certain details were withheld.

What James Risen learned in the course of his reporting can be found in his *State of War: The Secret History of the CIA and the Bush Administration*,[1] a wide-ranging investigation of the role of

---

1. Free Press, 2006.

intelligence in the origins and the conduct of the war in Iraq. Risen contributes much new material to our knowledge of recent intelligence history. He reports in detail, for example, on claims that CIA analysts quit fighting over exaggerated reports of Iraqi weapons of mass destruction as word spread in the corridors at Langley that the president had decided to go to war no matter what the evidence said; that the Saudi government seized and then got rid of tell-tale bank records of Abu Zubaydah, the most important al-Qaeda figure to be captured since September 11; and that "a handful of the most important al Qaeda detainees" have been sent for interrogation to a secret prison codenamed "Bright Light." One CIA specialist in counterterror operations told Risen, "The word is that once you get sent to Bright Light, you never come back."

Digging out intelligence history is a slow process, resisted by officials at every step of the way, and Risen's work will be often quoted in future accounts of the Iraq war. But nothing else in Risen's book rivals the NSA story in importance, revealing that the president authorized the NSA not only to eavesdrop on Americans without seeking court orders, but to listen in a new way, by intercepting a large volume of communications among categories of people, and then analyzing or "mining" the data in those calls for suspicious patterns that might offer "potential evidence of terrorist activity."

"This is the biggest secret I know about," one official told Risen. The eavesdropping effort is technically known as a "special access program" (SAP), which means that its existence and the information it collects are both tightly held. Within the government, Risen tells us, witting officials referred to it simply as "the program," and even the legal opinions justifying it are classified. Risen traces the origins of the program back to the brief war that overthrew the Taliban government in Afghanistan and resulted in the capture of many al-Qaeda suspects along with their cell phones and computers. These suspects had been calling and e-mailing people throughout the world, many of whom, inevitably, were in the United States, raising understandable fears of new terrorist attacks. But according to Risen, the NSA does not limit itself to monitoring numbers provided by the CIA from captured al-Qaeda phone books, targets for which there is some degree of "probable cause" to think they might be terrorist-connected. Those phone numbers provide only the jumping-off point for the program. The NSA has since broadened its effort by establishing "its own internal checklist" to pinpoint phone numbers and addresses of interest, and it is likely that the items on the list are checked off by a computer program in a nanosecond, not by analysts exercising deliberate judgment.

How big is the target list? At any given moment, Risen believes, the NSA may be "eavesdropping on as many as five hundred people in the United States." But his number of five hundred should not be interpreted as an outer limit. The actual volume of intercepted calls is almost certainly a very great deal larger, going beyond communications between known, named persons. Modern eavesdropping seldom mirrors the classic wiretap of yesteryear when FBI agents with earphones might record hundreds of hours of a Mafia chief chatting with his underboss in New York's Little Italy. The idea now is to see if *anyone* on the phone in New York or New Jersey sounds in any way like a Mafia chief. A dinner of linguine with clams in a known Mafia hangout could be enough to warrant a further look. The al-Qaeda phone book numbers were the crack in the door; follow-up targets are simply numbers or e-mail addresses, leading to other numbers and e-mail addresses, all plucked from the torrents of traffic transmitted by the switching systems of the major American telecommunications companies, which daily handle two billion phone calls and perhaps ten times as many e-mail messages. What Risen discovered, in short, was a program best described as "big."

Under existing law the NSA should have sought permission from the secret FISA court in Washington before listening in on the communications of any "US persons"—basically, American corporations, citizens, and others lawfully inside the United States— who had turned up in al-Qaeda phone books and directories. The law makes provision for emergencies: if investigators feel they don't have time for legal rigmarole they can act first and then seek permission within the following three days. This was not done. President Bush insisted on New Year's Day 2006 that "this is a limited program...it's limited to calls from outside the United States to calls within the United States. But they are of known—numbers of known al-Qaeda members or affiliates." But it seems clear that the NSA program quickly spilled beyond its original limits; the real reason for ignoring the FISA courts is probably a savvy guess that the courts would not approve what the administration wants to do.

Listening to specific persons was only part of it, and not the greater part. What Risen learned, which has been backed up by other press accounts in recent weeks, is that the counterterror investigators from the beginning wanted to cast the net wide—to listen to all the people in the al-Qaeda phone books, and then broaden their search to the still wider circle of people the phone book names were in touch with, and go on to check out all *their* contacts as well. If the first generation of targets numbered a hundred, let's say, and each of them had been talking to a hundred people in a second generation of targets, then even a third-generation search could easily sweep up a million people. You can see why investigators desperate to prevent any repetition of the attacks of September 11 would have favored this rapid and wide casting of the net, but that sort of industrial-scale fishing expedition is exactly what the FISA courts were established to prevent.

In the days after the Risen–Lichtblau story first appeared, President Bush, Attorney General Alberto Gonzales, the head of the NSA at the beginning of the program, General Michael Hayden, and others all defended the program as urgent, successful, justified by acts of Congress and the president's powers under the Constitution, sharply limited in scope, approved by members of Congress who had been briefed on the program, and carefully managed to protect the civil liberties and other rights of Americans.

"The whole key here is agility," said General Hayden.

"What we're trying to do is learn of communications, back and forth, from within the United States to overseas members of al-Qaeda," said Gonzales. "That's what this program is about. This is not about wiretapping everybody. This is about a very concentrated, very limited program focused on gaining information about our enemy."

"Dealing with al-Qaeda is not simply a matter of law enforcement," President Bush said in a press conference on December 19, 2005.

> It requires defending the country against an enemy that declared war against the United States.... So, consistent with US law and the Constitution, I authorized the interception of international communications of people with known links to al-Qaeda and related terrorist organizations.... Leaders in the United States Congress have been briefed more than a dozen times on this program.... I've reauthorized this program more than 30 times since the September the 11th attacks, and I intend to do so for so long as...the nation faces the continuing threat....

The president's carefully worded statement casts a troubling new light on his insistence that we are fighting a "war on terror" and that he is a "wartime president." Constitutional lawyers have long argued about the limits of presidential or executive power, but all agree that the limits are more elastic in wartime, and it is increasingly evident that the Bush administration has treated this distinction as a barn door. The shock caused by the revelation of the NSA program is not centered on concern for the civil liberties of al-Qaeda terrorists but on the scale, still unknown, of the eavesdropping authorized by the president; on his refusal to use the courts or seek any change in the governing laws; and on his blanket claim that Article Two of the Constitution gives him, as president and commander in chief of the armed forces, both the responsibility for defending the country and "the authority necessary to fulfill it."

Even some Republican leaders find this broad claim troubling. Senator Arlen Specter, chairman of the Senate's Judiciary Committee, said he planned to hold hearings on the NSA program. "I am skeptical of the attorney general's citation of authority, but I am prepared to listen," he said in December. "You can't have the administration and a select number of members [of Congress, those briefed by the White House] alter the law. It can't be done."

In an interview with Fox News on January 19, 2006, Vice President Dick Cheney said such briefings "have occurred at least a dozen times. I presided over most of them." One of those briefings, possibly the first, was held in Vice President Cheney's office on July 17, 2003, four months after the American invasion of Iraq and a year after the NSA program began. Present were Representatives Jane Harman and Porter Goss, later the director of the CIA; and Senators Pat Roberts and John D. Rockefeller. Briefing them were Goss's predecessor at the CIA, George Tenet, and General Hayden of the NSA. There has been no published account of what the members of Congress were told about the nature, rationale, justification, and scale of the program. They were permitted neither to take notes nor to discuss what they heard with any other persons. Far from feeling that the administration had fulfilled its obligations under existing law, Senator Rockefeller handwrote a brief letter to Cheney the same day

> to reiterate my concern regarding the sensitive intelligence issues we discussed today.... Clearly, the activities we discussed raise profound oversight issues.... Given the security restrictions associated with this information, and my inability to

consult staff or counsel on my own, I feel unable to fully evaluate, much less endorse these activities. As I reflected on the meeting today, and the future we face, John Poindexter's TIA project sprung to mind, exacerbating my concern. . . .

TIA stands for Total Information Awareness, an intelligence program conceived in the Pentagon's Defense Advanced Research Projects Agency (DARPA) in the year following the attacks of September 11. It was designed to collect and exploit digital records of all kinds from private and public compilers of information—phone records, bank records, credit card records, police records, medical records, travel records—basically everything that is recorded about individuals. Running the program was John Poindexter, a former Navy admiral and national security adviser under President Reagan who had been indicted and convicted on seven felony charges during the Iran-contra investigation in the early 1990s, convictions later overturned on appeal. When *The New York Times* first published a description of TIA in December 2002, the fact that Poindexter was running it proved a fatal debility, and in September 2003 Congress killed funding for the Pentagon's Information Awareness Office.

But Poindexter's retirement and the end of the IAO did not extinguish official hopes for "data mining," a computer-intensive approach to finding meaning in apparently random patterns. This, in fact, is basically what the NSA has always done—collect communications from targets of interest and attack them with "tools," which are basically computer programs that seek patterns in apparently random letter and number groups. Data mining seeks patterns in random actions—buying, selling, check writing, getting on planes, and so on—rather than in the numbers and letters that make up codes. Data mining is not a way to find out what persons of interest have been up to; it is a way to identify persons of interest among the general population—persons, in short, who have not been detected doing anything that might convince a judge on the FISA court to issue a warrant for surveillance. Checking out US persons contacted by al-Qaeda would have raised no red flags with FISA judges; the larger and more significant part of the program uncovered by James Risen—the part which the administration did not want to describe to the FISA court or to members of Congress who could have amended the law; the part, in fact, which the administration still hopes to keep secret and continue —is the use of data-mining techniques by the NSA to do what Congress refused to allow Poindexter and the Pentagon to do. And that is to generate large numbers of names—not dozens, thousands—for the FBI to investigate.

John Poindexter and Total Information Awareness were one bell that rang loudly in the mind of Senator Rockefeller after his briefing in Cheney's office. It is probable that another has rung since—the testimony of John Bolton during his confirmation hearings in 2005 to be US ambassador to the UN, when he said that on ten occasions he had formally asked the NSA to identify the "US persons" who had been party to, or perhaps only mentioned in, communications intercepted by the agency and included in reports distributed to others in the government. The fight over the administration's refusal to identify the nineteen persons who aroused Bolton's curiosity in those ten communications was one reason President Bush abandoned efforts to force a Senate vote and instead made an interim appointment of Bolton to the UN post while Congress was in recess. But the argument while it continued jarred loose additional information about the scale of NSA activity—for example, the State Department's admission that Bolton's colleagues had made over four hundred requests for the identities of US persons in NSA reports; that the NSA had been asked as many as 3,500 times by other agencies to fill in the names of US persons, and that the total number of names provided to other agencies was greater than 10,000.

Who are these people? Some of them were probably included in a database of 1,519 "suspicious incidents" compiled by the Pentagon's Counterintelligence Field Activity, an office charged with defending military bases, according to a report broadcast by NBC a few days before the original *New York Times* story on the NSA program. On examination, the Pentagon's "suspicious incidents" were simply public protests of the sort watched, photographed, investigated, and wiretapped during the Vietnam War under the program that led to the enactment of FISA twenty-five years ago. At that time the Pentagon's database had ballooned to 18,000 names.

Of the numerous questions facing investigators for the Judiciary Committee, the easy ones will concern the legality of the program. It was patently illegal under FISA and the only argument for letting the president get away with ignoring FISA is that he is prepared to make a fight of it. No committee headed by Republicans will do more than chide him on the law. The questions hardest to answer will be what the NSA actually did, and whether it served any useful purpose. A *New York Times* story in late 2005 contradicts the president's claim that the NSA program was "limited...to known al-Qaeda members or affiliates." Citing anonymous FBI officials, the *Times* claimed that the NSA flooded the bureau with "thousands" of names per month to check out for possible terrorist connections. Far from being a "vital tool," as described by President Bush, the program was a distracting time waster that sent harried FBI agents down an endless series of blind alleys chasing will-o'-the-wisp terrorists who turned out to be schoolteachers. And far from saving "thousands of lives," as claimed by Vice President Dick Cheney in December 2005, the NSA program never led investigators to a genuine terrorist not already under suspicion, nor did it help them to expose any dangerous plots. So why did the administration continue this lumbering effort for three years? Outsiders sometimes find it tempting to dismiss such wheel-spinning as bureaucratic silliness, but I believe that the Judiciary Committee will find, if it is willing to persist, that within the large pointless program there exists a small, sharply focused program that delivers something the White House really wants. This it will never confess willingly.

Over the next few months the White House will be fighting a two-front war to preserve its secrets—one against the Judiciary Committee, as just described, and a second against the Senate Intelligence Committee, which has committed itself to a renewed effort to investigate the administration's drum-beating for war with Iraq by citing scary reports of Saddam Hussein's weapons of mass destruction—reports that were virtually all wrong, and in some cases were little short of fabricated.

The committee's chairman, Senator Pat Roberts, promised before the 2004 presidential election that "phase two" of its investigation would address the administration's actual use of the intelligence it received, flawed as it was. This was something of a minefield. On their face, many statements by Bush, Cheney, National Security Adviser Condoleezza Rice, and Secretary of Defense Donald Rumsfeld appeared to go well beyond even the exaggerated claims made by the CIA. After Bush won a second term, the Republican Roberts not surprisingly dropped "phase two," saying he no longer saw the point. But in November 2005 Senator Harry Reid, a Democrat on the Senate Intelligence Committee, revived phase two when he invoked a rarely used parliamentary rule to call for a secret session of the Senate to discuss new evidence suggesting that substantial doubts about WMD intelligence had been suppressed before the war.

Risen found evidence of that, too. Included in his book is a new account of a pre-war CIA program conceived by the agency's assistant director for intelligence collection, Charles Allen, to send Iraqi-Americans to Baghdad to ask scientist-relatives about WMDs. A chief target of the new program was Iraq's effort to develop nuclear weapons, the subject of intense ongoing scrutiny after a son-in-law of

Saddam Hussein defected in mid-1995 to Amman, Jordan, where he described WMD programs to UN officials. Sawsan Alhaddad, a woman doctor working and living in Cleveland, was one of about thirty Iraqis dispatched to Baghdad under this program in late summer 2002. When she returned in September she told CIA debriefers in a Virginia hotel room that her brother, an electrical engineer who had joined the Iraqi nuclear program in the early 1980s, had insisted the nuclear weapons program was dead, shut down years earlier. The other Iraqis all said the same thing only months before the US invasion of Iraq in March 2003, but their reports were bottled up in the CIA.

The agency, it turns out, had heard the same thing from many sources, including Hussein's defector son-in-law, General Hussein Kamal, who was fool enough to return to Baghdad, where he was executed. But before leaving, Kamal told the UN that Iraq's WMD program, larger and more advanced than the CIA had believed before the first Gulf War in 1991, had been closed down

> after visits of [UN] inspection teams. You have important role in Iraq with this. You should not underestimate yourself. You are very effective in Iraq.... All chemical weapons were destroyed. I ordered destruction of all chemical weapons. All weapons— biological, chemical, missile, nuclear were destroyed.... In the nuclear area, there were no weapons. Missile and chemical weapons were real weapons. Our main worry was Iran and they were [intended for use] against them.

Kamal's report, like Sawsan Alhaddad's and many others, was never cited in the October 2002 National Intelligence Estimate used to convince Congress to vote for war. The pattern is clear; evidence of Iraqi WMDs, however flimsy, was treated like scripture while information contradicting that evidence, however clear, was bottled up and never left the building. On three separate occasions, for example, in mid-2001, mid-2002, and January 2003, just before the war, the CIA asked the French for their evaluation of the now infamous reports that Iraq was trying to buy "yellowcake" uranium ore from Niger. According to the *Los Angeles Times* of December 11, 2005, the French intelligence chief at the time, Alain Chouet, said that the answer was the same in each instance—nothing to it.

The French were in a position to know; uranium ore in Niger was all mined by French companies. In mid-2002 the French even told the CIA that the Italian documents reporting the purchase were forgeries, something the CIA did not even attempt to examine on its own for another year; and a few months later, "at about the same time as the State of the Union address" when the president cited the yellowcake purchase as alarming evidence of Saddam Hussein's nuclear ambitions, the Italians also told the Americans that the documents were forgeries. In similar fashion, claims that Iraq was providing al-Qaeda with training in the use of poison gases, cited by Secretary of State Colin Powell at the UN in February 2003, were also contradicted by reports the CIA had but chose to ignore.

In public debate it is customary at this point to ask, in a voice of amazed horror, How could this have happened? Are these intelligence professionals all community college dropouts? Have they forgotten everything they learned in spy school? My own view is that inconvenient evidence that angers policymakers and threatens careers cannot be pushed under the rug by intelligence officers unless they are fully aware of each step in the series— they know it is evidence, they know it is inconvenient, they know it will anger policymakers, they know their careers will be threatened, and they know they are pushing evidence in the direction of a rug.

James Risen is not willing to go so far. His book is filled with evidence supporting this interpretation, but he seems reluctant to embrace it. "[Paul] Wolfowitz personally complained to Tenet about the CIA's analytical work on Iraq and al-Qaeda," Risen says in discussing the

use of intelligence to justify the war. Can we be in doubt why Wolfowitz complained, or why the agency assured Powell that Iraq was
training al-Qaeda, scout's honor? When CIA officers told Tenet the
war would be a mistake, Risen notes, "he would just come back from
the White House and say they are going to do it." Risen sums up
Tenet's attitude thus: "War with Iraq was inevitable, and it was time
for the CIA to do its part." That seems clear enough; surely Risen
means that the agency's part was to help beat the drum for war. But
then Risen swings back, like a man facing snakes on one side and alli-
gators on the other. Why was the information reported by Sawsan
Alhaddad and the other Iraqis bottled up at the agency? "Petty turf
battles and tunnel vision of the agency's officials" is Risen's first
answer. In the next sentence he braces up, then wilts again:

> ...Doubts were stifled because of the enormous pressure that
> officials at the CIA...felt to support the administration. CIA
> director George Tenet and his senior lieutenants became
> so...fearful of creating a rift with the White House, that they
> created a climate within the CIA in which warnings that the
> available evidence on Iraqi WMD was weak were either ignored
> or censored. Tenet and his senior aides may not have meant to
> foster that sort of work environment—and perhaps did not even
> realize they were doing it....

What can Risen be thinking? How could they not realize they were
doing it? They were running the place.

Paul Wolfowitz, the undersecretary of defense, was not the only
official to let the CIA know what he wanted to hear. Rumsfeld set up a
special office in the Pentagon to "re-look" the intelligence on Iraqi
WMDs and then urged Tenet to listen to its findings. Vice President
Cheney crossed the Potomac more than once to ask questions—the
same questions, over and over. John Bolton tried to fire resistant ana-

lysts in the State Department's intelligence shop and at the CIA; they kept their jobs, but who could fail to get the message? Robert Hutchings, a former chief of the National Intelligence Council, the group that wrote the October 2002 NIE, described Bolton's way of mining intelligence reports to come up with the administration's version of the world. "He took isolated facts and made much more to build a case than the intelligence warranted," he said. "It was a sort of cherry-picking of little factoids and little isolated bits that were drawn out to present the starkest-possible case."

These were not intellectual exercises; Bolton needed custom-built intelligence to support the administration's policies. "When policy officials came back repeatedly to push the same kind of judgments, and push the intelligence community to confirm a particular set of judgments," Hutchings said, "it does have the effect of politicizing intelligence, because the so-called 'correct answer' becomes all too clear."[2] Has the Senate Intelligence Committee got the fortitude to accept the implications of these facts and many others just like them?

The systematic exaggeration of intelligence before the invasion of Iraq and the flouting of FISA both required, and got, a degree of resolution in the White House that has few precedents in American history. The president has gotten away with it so far because he leaves no middle ground—cut him some slack, or prepare to fight to the death. The fact that he enjoys a Republican majority in both houses of Congress gives him a margin of comfort, but I suspect that Democratic majorities would be just as reluctant, in the end, to call him on either count. Americans were ready enough to believe that one president might lie about a sexual affair; but they balk at concluding that his successor would pressure others to lie, and even would utter a few whoppers himself, so he could take the country to war.

Risen helps to explain how it was done, but lets it go at that. In his

---

2. *Arms Control Today*, June 2005.

Fox News interview Vice President Cheney did not give an inch on the necessity of the NSA spying or of the war itself. "When we look back on this, ten years hence," he insisted, "we will [see that we] have fundamentally changed the course of history in that part of the world." A decade down the road we'll know if Cheney is right or wrong, and if the change is the one we wanted. The question now is whether the president could do it all again—take the country to war, and scrap restraints on spying, just as he pleases. The answer is yes, unless Congress and the courts can say no.

—*The New York Review of Books*, February 23, 2006

8

WHAT TENET KNEW

HOW WE GOT INTO IRAQ is the great open question of the decade but George Tenet in *At the Center of the Storm: My Years at the* CIA,[1] his memoir of his seven years running the Central Intelligence Agency, takes his sweet time working his way around to it. He hesitates because he has much to explain: the claims made by Tenet's CIA with "high confidence" that Iraq was dangerously armed all proved false. But mistakes are one thing, excusable even when serious; inexcusable would be charges of collusion in deceiving Congress and the public to make war possible. Tenet's overriding goal in his carefully written book is to deny "that we somehow cooked the books" about Iraq's weapons of mass destruction. If he says it once he says it a dozen times. "We told the president what we did on Iraq WMD because we believed it."

But repetition is not enough. Tenet's problem is that the intelligence and the war proceeded in lockstep: no intelligence, no war. Since Tenet delivered the (shockingly exaggerated) intelligence, and the president used it to go to war, how is Tenet to convince the world that he wasn't simply giving the boss what he wanted? Tenet naturally dislikes this question but it is evident that the American public and Congress dislike it just as much. Down that road lie painful truths

---

1. HarperCollins, 2007.

about the character and motives of the president and the men and women around him. But getting out of Iraq will not be easy, and the necessary first step is to find the civic courage to insist on knowing how we got in. Tenet's memoir is an excellent place to begin; some of what he tells us and much that he leaves out point unmistakably to the genesis of the war in the White House—the very last thing Tenet wants to address clearly. He sidles up to the question at last on page 301: "One of the great mysteries to me," he writes, "is exactly when the war in Iraq became inevitable."

Hans Blix, director of the United Nations weapons inspection team, did not believe that war was inevitable until the shooting started. In Blix's view, reported in his memoir *Disarming Iraq*,[2] the failure of his inspectors to find Saddam Hussein's WMDs meant that a US invasion of Iraq could certainly be put off, perhaps avoided altogether. For Blix it was all about the weapons. Tenet's version of events makes it clear that WMDs, despite all the ballyhoo, were in fact secondary; something else was driving events. Tenet's omissions begin on Day Two of the march to war, September 12, 2001, when three British officials came to CIA headquarters "just for the night, to express their condolences and to be with us. We had dinner that night at Langley...as touching an event as I experienced during my seven years as DCI." This would have been an excellent place to describe the genesis of the war but Tenet declines. We must fill in the missing pieces ourselves.

The guests that night were David Manning, barely a week into his new job as Tony Blair's personal foreign policy adviser; Richard Dearlove, chief of the British secret intelligence service known as MI6, a man Tenet already knew well; and Eliza Manningham-Buller, the deputy chief of MI5, the British counterpart to the FBI. Despite the ban on air traffic, Dearlove and Manningham-Buller had flown into Andrews Air Force Base near Washington that day.

---

2. Pantheon, 2004.

But David Manning was already inside the United States. The day before the attack on the World Trade Center, on September 10, he had been in Washington for a dinner with Condoleezza Rice at the home of the British ambassador, Christopher Meyer. Early on September 11 Manning took the shuttle to New York and from his airplane window on the approach to Kennedy Airport he saw smoke rising from one of the World Trade Center towers. By the time he landed the second tower had been struck. It took a full day for the British embassy to fetch Manning back to Washington by car, and he arrived at Langley that night carrying the burden of what he had seen. It was a largish group that gathered for dinner. Along with the three British guests and Tenet were Jim Pavitt and his deputy at the CIA's Directorate for Operations; Tenet's executive director, Buzzy Krongard; the chief of the Counter Terrorism Center, Cofer Black; the acting director of the FBI, Thomas Pickard; the chief of the CIA's Near East Division, still not identified; and the chief of the CIA's European Division, Tyler Drumheller.

Tenet names his British guests, but omits all that was said. Tyler Drumheller, barred by the CIA from identifying the visitors in his own recent memoir, *On the Brink*, reports an exchange between Manning and Tenet, who were probably meeting for the first time.

"I hope we can all agree," said Manning, "that we should concentrate on Afghanistan and not be tempted to launch any attacks on Iraq."

"Absolutely," Tenet replied, "we all agree on that. Some might want to link the issues, but none of us wants to go that route."[3]

Manning already understood that people close to President Bush wanted to go after Iraq, and Tenet of course knew it too. Conspicuous among them, in his mind that night, was the neoconservative

---

3. Tyler Drumheller with Elaine Monaghan, *On the Brink: An Insider's Account of How the White House Compromised American Intelligence* (Carroll and Graf, 2006), p. 31.

agitator and polemicist Richard Perle, an outspoken advocate of removing Saddam Hussein by military force. On the very first page of Tenet's memoir, he tells us that he had run into Perle that very morning—September 12—as Perle was leaving the West Wing of the White House. They knew each other in a passing way, as figures of note on the Washington scene. As Tenet reached the door Perle turned to him and said, "Iraq has to pay a price for what happened yesterday. They bear responsibility."

This made a powerful impression on the director of the CIA:

> I was stunned but said nothing.... At the Secret Service security checkpoint, I looked back at Perle and thought: What the hell is he talking about? Moments later, a second thought came to me: Who has Richard Perle been meeting with in the White House so early in the morning on today of all days? I never learned the answer to that question.[4]

The meeting with Perle and the dinner with Manning and Dearlove took place on Wednesday. On Saturday, Tenet was at Camp David where President Bush was weighing the American response to the attacks of September 11. During the discussion, arguments for removing Saddam were pressed by Paul Wolfowitz, another neoconservative and longtime friend of Perle who was the deputy secretary of defense under Donald Rumsfeld. "The president listened to Paul's views," Tenet writes, "but, fairly quickly, it seemed to me, dismissed them." The vote against including Iraq "in our immediate response plans" was four to zero against, with Rumsfeld abstaining. Tenet adds, "I recall no mention of WMD."

---

4. Perle denies seeing Tenet that day, and Tenet concedes he may have been off by a day or two; but Tenet says he was not wrong about Perle's remark. In his mind as he wrote his memoirs, however, Tenet remembered Perle's remark and the visit by Manning as bookending the same day.

Four days later, at a meeting in the White House, Bush made a request of Tenet. Through a video hookup Vice President Dick Cheney was in the room as well. "I want to know about links between Saddam and al Qaeda," said the President. "The Vice President knows some things that might be helpful."[5]

What the Vice President thought he knew was that one of the September 11 hijackers, Mohamed Atta, had met in Prague earlier in the year with an official of Iraqi intelligence. Tenet responded within days to say that evidence from phone calls and credit cards demonstrated that Atta was in the United States at the time of the alleged meeting, living in a Virginia apartment not far from the CIA. A proven link between Saddam and September 11 would have ended the debate about "regime change" right there. None was ever established, then or later, but Cheney and his personal national security adviser, I. Lewis Libby, known by his nickname as Scooter, argued and reargued the case for the link until the eve of war. Often they went to the agency personally, bringing fresh allegations acquired from their own sources, and pressing CIA analysts to "re-look" the evidence. Under continuing White House pressure the agency treated their claims respectfully. Analysts conceded that "cooperation, safe haven, training, and reciprocal nonaggression" were all discussed by al-Qaeda and Iraqi officials. "But operational direction and control?" Tenet asks. "No."

The Vice President did not take no for an answer. He often cited the link in public and he wanted the CIA to back him up. In June 2002, the deputy director for intelligence, Jami Miscik, complained to Tenet that Scooter Libby and Paul Wolfowitz would not let the subject drop. Tenet reports that he told Miscik to "just say 'we stand by what we previously wrote.'" But six months later, in January

---

5. This story is told by Ron Suskind in his book *The One Percent Doctrine: Deep Inside America's Pursuit of Its Enemies Since 9/11* (Simon and Schuster, 2006), p. 23, which is evidently based on interviews with Tenet and Tenet's close aides in the CIA.

2003, Stephen Hadley at the National Security Council summoned Miscik to the White House for yet another revision of a "link" paper. Infuriated, Miscik went to Tenet's office and told him she would resign before she would change another word. Tenet says he called Hadley. "'Steve,' I said, 'knock this off. The paper is done.... Jami is not coming down there to discuss it anymore.'"

Ron Suskind tells the same story but quotes Tenet differently on the phone to Hadley: "It is fucking over. Do you hear me! And don't you ever fucking treat my people this way again. Ever!"

Even that was not the end. In mid-March 2003, less than a week before the US launched its attack, Cheney sent a speech over to the CIA for review making all the old arguments that there was a "link." Tenet tells us that he telephoned Bush to say, "The vice president wants to make a speech about Iraq and al-Qa'ida that goes way beyond what the intelligence shows. We cannot support the speech, and it should not be given."

Why did Cheney press this point so relentlessly? Tenet tells a story that helps to explain the motives behind the struggle over "intelligence" between September 11 and the day American cruise missiles began to land on Baghdad, eighteen months later. Only a few days after September 11, Tenet writes, a CIA analyst attended a White House meeting where he was told that Bush wanted to remove Saddam. The analyst's response, according to Tenet:

> If you want to go after that son of a bitch to settle old scores, be my guest. But don't tell us he is connected to 9/11 or to terrorism because there is no evidence to support that. You will have to have a better reason.

The better reason eventually settled on by President Bush was Saddam Hussein's weapons of mass destruction. The evidence for WMDs turned out to be even weaker than the evidence for "the link," but

Cheney, with the full backing of the White House and the National Security Council, hammered without let-up on the horrific consequences of error—discovering too late that Iraq had nuclear weapons meant that the smoking gun would be a mushroom cloud. It was vaguely believed at the time, by the public and foreign intelligence services alike, that the CIA must have learned something new; why else in early 2002 had Saddam Hussein suddenly become a threat to the world?

In fact only one thing had changed—the American frame of mind, something clearly understood by advisers to Britain's Tony Blair, who had decided immediately after September 11 that he was going to back the American response, whatever it was. David Manning's hope, expressed at his dinner with Tenet, that the Americans would settle for the invasion of Afghanistan and the overthrow of the Taliban was soon dashed. A week later Tony Blair himself was at the White House. Bush took him immediately by the elbow, according to the British ambassador, Christopher Meyer, and moved the prime minister off into a corner of the room.

Don't get distracted, Blair told the President; Taliban first.

"I agree with you, Tony," Bush replied. "We must deal with this first. But when we have dealt with Afghanistan, we must come back to Iraq."

The Taliban were in retreat by the end of the year; on March 1, Robert Einhorn, an assistant secretary of state for nonproliferation, testified in Congress that Bush had come back to Iraq: "A consensus seems to be developing in Washington in favor of 'regime change' in Iraq, if necessary through the use of military force."

As it happened, it took a year to get from point A to point B—from developing consensus to war. During that year George Tenet's CIA played an indispensable part in raising fears of Saddam Hussein's weapons of mass destruction, but in his memoir Tenet is reluctant to approach the Iraq problem. He writes proudly of the agency's success in removing the Taliban—which was in fact a marvel of the light touch, especially in retrospect—and insists he was slow to recognize that Iraq was next:

> My many sleepless nights back then didn't center on Saddam Hussein. Al-Qa'ida occupied my nightmares.... Looking back, I wish I could have devoted equal energy and attention to Iraq.... Iraq deserved more of my time. But the simple fact is that I didn't see that freight train coming as early as I should have.

When did war become inevitable? When did Tenet see the freight train coming? Does he really hope to convince us that it took him longer than the British, who signed on for war at a meeting with Bush at his Texas ranch in April 2002?

What we know about the extraordinarily close British–American relationship in the run-up to war comes mainly from a series of high-level British government papers known collectively as "the Downing Street memos."[6] An unknown person gave them to the British newspaper correspondent Michael Smith—a first batch of six, in September 2004, when Smith was working for the *Telegraph*; and two more the following May after Smith had moved over to the London *Times*. These documents reveal British plans in a language of bald directness and candor. There is no fudge; there is no evasion of awkward fact; there is frank admission of where they want to get and how they plan to get there.

The British had no objection to overthrowing Saddam by military means but feared that the American willingness to go it alone would undermine the case, anger the world, and make it impossible for Britain to take part. The solution was to cast Saddam as the villain,

---

6. Mark Danner, *The Secret Way to War: The Downing Street Memo and the Iraq War's Buried History* (New York Review Books, 2006).

and the British saw promise in his serial rejection of UN resolutions. If he could be coaxed to defy one last and final offer to disarm, worded carefully to make UN demands sound fair, then the world might come around to seeing war as reasonable. This was the strategy the British hoped to sell to the Americans in the spring of 2002. In a first step, David Manning in mid-March flew again to Washington where he met twice with the national security adviser, Condoleezza Rice. He reported in a memo to Blair on March 14:

> These were good exchanges, and particularly frank when we were one-on-one at dinner.... Condi's enthusiasm for regime change is undimmed. But there were some signs, since we last spoke, of greater awareness of the practical difficulties.... From what she said, Bush has yet to find the answers to the big questions: how to persuade international opinion that military action against Iraq is necessary and justified;...what happens on the morning after?

Blair was in a strong position, in Manning's view. "Bush will want to pick your brains," he told the prime minister in his memo. "He also wants your support." The price of that support, Manning told Rice, would be recognition of British concerns—

> in particular: the UN dimension. The issue of the weapons inspectors must be handled in a way that would persuade European and wider opinion that the US was conscious of the international framework, and the insistence of many countries on the need for a legal base. Renewed refusal by Saddam to accept unfettered inspections would be a powerful argument.

A few days after Manning's dinner with Rice, Christopher Meyer invited Paul Wolfowitz to lunch at the ambassador's residence. He reported the result to Manning on March 18: "I opened by sticking very closely to the script that you used with Condi Rice last week." Yes, Britain supported regime change but the world had to be brought along. Wolfowitz wanted to talk about Saddam's crimes and his connections to al-Qaeda—"did we, he asked, know anything more about this meeting" of Mohamed Atta with the Iraqi intelligence officer in Prague? Meyer stuck to the script: "I then went through the need to wrongfoot Saddam on the inspectors and the UNSCRs [Security Council resolutions]...."[7]

The British foreign secretary, Jack Straw, expanded on this argument in his options paper for Blair at the end of the month. Making the case, in Straw's view, meant going back to the UN:

> That Iraq is in flagrant breach of international legal obligations imposed on it by UNSC provides us with the core of a strategy.... I believe that a demand for the unfettered readmission of weapons inspectors is essential, in terms of public explanation, and in terms of legal sanction for any subsequent military action.

Straw appended a memo from the Foreign Office political director, Peter Ricketts, who described the immediate challenge as explaining why Iraq, and why now?

> The truth is that...even the best survey of Iraq's WMD programmes will not show much advance in recent years on the nuclear, missile or CW/BW fronts: the programmes are extremely worrying but have not, as far as we know, been stepped up.... We are still left with a problem of bringing public opinion to accept the imminence of a threat from Iraq. This is something

7. Danner, *The Secret Way to War*, p. 134.

the Prime Minister and President need to have a frank discussion about.

Blair met with Bush in Crawford, Texas, on April 6 and promised to join a military campaign for Saddam's removal, but only, Blair stressed, after "the options for action to eliminate Iraq's WMD through the UN weapons inspectors had been exhausted." Bush did not say yes to this at the time and as spring of 2002 moved into summer the Vice President argued against any return to the UN. Cheney feared that Baghdad would renew its cat-and-mouse game with inspectors, the process would drag on, and the administration's determination to invade and occupy Iraq would gradually erode, leaving a defiant Saddam still in power.

The British made a final effort to convince Bush to obtain a UN resolution in July, beginning with a trip to Washington by MI6's director, Richard Dearlove, to check the temperature of American thinking. On Saturday, July 20, Dearlove and other British intelligence officials visited the CIA in Langley, where George Tenet took Dearlove aside for a private talk that lasted an hour and a half. On July 23, back in London, Dearlove reported on his frank discussions in Washington.

But first let us consider Tenet's account of this episode in his memoir. It is deceptive in the extreme. "In May of 2002," he writes, Dearlove came to Washington and met with Rice, Hadley, Scooter Libby, and Congressman Porter Goss, then chair of the House Intelligence Committee. Three years later the documents leaked to the British press quoted Dearlove describing his findings in Washington at a cabinet meeting. Tenet writes, "Sir Richard later told me that he had been misquoted."

May of 2002? Tenet is off by two months. I suspect that Dearlove really did come in May as well, and that Tenet cites the earlier visit to muddy the waters about his meeting with Dearlove on July 20—neither denying it took place nor lying about what was said. After May

2005—a full year after Tenet had left the CIA—Dearlove "told me that he had been misquoted." Tenet knows what he told Dearlove; does he think his views were misrepresented by Dearlove's report to the cabinet, as recorded in the minutes? Tenet does not say. He adds that Dearlove "believed that the crowd around the vice president was playing fast and loose with the evidence." In short, Tenet is trying to put a country mile of daylight between Dearlove's unvarnished report to the British cabinet and Tenet's ninety-minute, private conversation with Dearlove at the CIA only three days earlier.

We may assume that the whole of Dearlove's remarks as reported in the cabinet meeting minutes were colored by what Tenet told him:

> C [the traditional designation for the chief of MI6] reported on his recent talks in Washington. There was a perceptible shift in attitude. Military action was now seen as inevitable. Bush wanted to remove Saddam, through military action, justified by the conjunction of terrorism and WMD. But the intelligence and facts were being fixed around the policy. The NSC had no patience with the UN route, and no enthusiasm for publishing material on the Iraqi regime's record. There was little discussion in Washington of the aftermath after military action.

Tenet has done his utmost—short of lying—to hide his role as Dearlove's informant, but every point the MI6 director made was something Tenet was uniquely positioned to tell him.

The danger from Blair's point of view was a bull-headed American drive to war which the British would find it politically impossible to join. He told the cabinet that "it would make a big difference politically and legally if Saddam refused to allow in the UN inspectors." The cabinet agreed that a strategy to "wrongfoot" Saddam through the UN was crucial. Jack Straw "would send the prime minister the background on the UN inspectors and discreetly work up the ultimatum to Saddam." Early in August Straw made a secret visit to argue Blair's case for the UN gambit with Secretary of State Colin Powell in the latter's house; Powell then pressed the point about the UN hard with Bush at a private White House dinner and Bush at last agreed. Tenet attended a final meeting on the issue at Camp David on Saturday morning, September 7:

> Colin Powell was firmly on the side of going the extra mile with the UN, while the vice president argued just as forcefully that doing so would only get us mired in a bureaucratic tangle with nothing to show for it other than the time lost off a ticking clock. The president let Powell and Cheney pretty much duke it out.

But the decision had already been made. Blair was also present at Camp David that day. He had been urging a UN resolution for months and had not crossed the ocean to be told no. According to Bob Woodward's book *Plan of Attack*, Bush told Blair that the United States would bring the question of Saddam's WMDs to the UN one more time before going to war, but war would probably still follow in the end.[8] Thus the stage was set for a UN melodrama starring a defiant Saddam before armies crossed borders, but nothing worked as the British had imagined. Saddam accepted unconditionally the Security Council's demand on November 8 for intrusive new inspections. While the report he submitted on Iraq's destruction of its WMDs was rejected as obfuscating, the UN was able to resume inspections at the end of November. Hans Blix's inspectors scoured the country inspecting hundreds of sites but found nothing, and Blix infuriated the White House by refusing to declare Iraq in material breach of Resolution 1441 demanding that he disarm.

As a ploy for war, "wrongfooting" Saddam was a bust. With each

---

8. Bob Woodward, *Plan of Attack* (Simon and Schuster), 2004, p. 178.

passing week he seemed less of a threat. Cheney's clock was ticking; American military plans, hoping to avoid the brutal Iraqi summer, called for fighting to begin in March at the latest. Bush was determined and Blair was willing to go forward with war, but since the UN gambit had generated no just cause for war, the Americans were compelled to make the case before the UN themselves. The date was set for February 5, and Colin Powell was chosen to present the evidence—the fruits of many months of work by the collectors and analysts of George Tenet's CIA. Everything seemed to rest on the strength of Powell's argument— the onset of war, the Bush policy to remake the Middle East, the American reputation in the world. This was the moment when the intelligence and the war fell completely into lockstep; no intelligence, no war. If Tenet is to be vindicated as an honest man this is where he must convince us the intelligence was genuinely believed and honestly presented.

"My colleagues," Powell said in the speech, "every statement I make today is backed up by sources, solid sources. These are not assertions. What we're giving you are facts and conclusions based on solid intelligence." Visible behind Powell as he placed his public reputation on the line was George Tenet, arms folded and filling his seat with bearlike bulk. Tenet had personally guaranteed Powell that every claim he made was on firm ground.

"It was a great presentation," Tenet writes of Powell's speech, "but unfortunately the substance didn't hold up."

The substance, in fact, was wrong in every particular, as is now well known. Tenet does not linger on that. He argues instead that it didn't matter: Bush didn't go to war because the CIA told him Saddam Hussein had WMDs—the dead-certain "slam dunk" he used to describe the evidence in a White House meeting in December 2002. And maybe the WMD claims in the agency's National Intelligence Estimate "were flawed," he writes, but didn't Congress have an obligation at the very least to read the whole of the ninety-page paper before voting to authorize war? Should their negligence be blamed on him? "The intelligence process was not disingenuous," he insists, "nor was it influenced by politics." This is the whole of his defense: we were wrong, but it was an honest error.

This is not the place for an exhaustive reexamination of the agency's long-exploded claims, but no plea of honest error can survive even a quick look at the facts in three disputes—what Iraq intended to do with aluminum tubes, how the agency knew about Iraq's mobile biological warfare labs, and why a report that Iraq was trying to buy uranium "yellowcake" in Niger made its way into one official speech after another until it finally appeared—the infamous "sixteen words"—in Bush's State of the Union speech in January 2003. None of these claims was robust when first encountered by the CIA. All were "processed" by CIA analysts in a manner intended to disguise shaky sources, minimize doubts, exclude alternative explanations, exaggerate their significance, and inflate the confidence level with which they were believed. None passes the "honest error" test.

After the seizure of a shipment of aluminum tubes bound for Iraq in the summer of 2001, a CIA analyst argued that they were intended for use in the building of centrifuges for separation of fissionable material, a claim rejected by experts for the Department of Energy when they learned of it. Analysts for the State Department also found the argument implausible. The CIA's view was leaked to a *New York Times* reporter in September 2002 and then cited the same day on a Sunday-morning talk show by Condoleezza Rice as proof sufficient of Saddam's nuclear plans unless we waited for "the smoking gun to be a mushroom cloud." The National Intelligence Estimate given to Congress at that time ignored Department of Energy objections and printed the State Department's footnote of protest sixty pages away from the bald claim that "all intelligence experts agree...that these tubes could be used in a centrifuge enrichment program." Only an elastic interpretation of the word "could" rescues this statement from being a bald lie. After a year of exhaustive postwar investigation, the

Iraq Survey Group concluded that the tubes were intended for use as battlefield rockets, as other experts and the Iraqi government had claimed all along.

In describing the Iraqi threat at the UN, Colin Powell laid it on thickest in his description of Iraq's mobile labs for the production of biological weapons, first reported by an Iraqi engineering student who defected to Germany in 1998 and was given the codename Curveball. German intelligence officials routinely passed on his claims to the Defense Intelligence Agency, which then circulated them to other American intelligence organizations in 2000 and 2001. Immediately after September 11 these reports became a major building block in the case for Iraqi WMDs, but the Germans refused access to Curveball, and later told the European Division chief, Tyler Drumheller, that Curveball was mentally unstable, that his reports had never been corroborated by anyone else, and that some German intelligence officials thought he was a fabricator.

In December 2002, while compiling evidence for Powell's speech to the UN, the CIA formally asked the Germans for permission to use Curveball's information. The German intelligence chief, August Hanning, wrote back on December 20 granting permission, but repeating what had been said to Drumheller two months earlier—Curveball's claims had never been corroborated. Tenet in his memoir denies that he saw Hanning's letter or was ever informed about the analysts' knockdown arguments over Curveball's claims. In one session, according to Drumheller, a Curveball believer insulted a Curveball doubter who responded, "You can kiss my ass in Macy's window." Drumheller comments, "It would be funny if it weren't so tragic."

But Tenet insists that word of the ruckus never reached him. Only a week before Powell's speech to the UN, the CIA's chief of station in Berlin cabled headquarters to say yet again that the Germans could not verify Curveball's claims, and adding:

Defer to headquarters but to use information from another liaison service's source whose information cannot be verified on such an important, key topic should take the most serious consideration.

Tenet has insisted that he never saw that cable either. Nor does he remember a last-minute warning from Drumheller the night before Powell's speech. Tenet had called Drumheller seeking a phone number. "As long as I've got you," said Drumheller on the phone, "there are some problems with the German reporting." Drumheller writes that he tried to tell Tenet that Curveball was worthless. Tenet remembers the phone call, but not the warning. What Curveball said was found by the Iraq Survey Group to be wrong in every detail.

The claim that Iraq was trying to buy yellowcake uranium in Niger was not only weak but was based, if that is the word, on evidence, if that is the word, that was fabricated in so obvious a manner that the CIA claims not to have seen the documents till very late in the day. First notice of the Iraqi–Niger connection reached the CIA shortly before September 11, probably from Italian intelligence officials passing on a two-year-old Telex which reported plans of the Iraqi ambassador to the Vatican to visit Niger. Two Italian journalists who have investigated the case, Carlo Bonini and Giuseppe D'Avanzo, note that the only significant Niger export is uranium ore. So this was an item of interest.

The uranium mines in Niger are under the control of a French company and the export of uranium ore is closely monitored by French intelligence, which answered a routine CIA query in the summer of 2001 by saying that nothing was amiss. The following spring the CIA was again "knocking on our door," according to Alain Chouet, the director of the French intelligence branch which monitors WMD matters. Chouet told Bonini and D'Avanzo, as they report in their book *Collusion: International Espionage and the War on Terror*, that there was now "an undeniable urgency" to American questions, which were no longer vague, but full of detail. Again the French investigated;

again the answer to the CIA was that nothing was amiss. But the Americans pressed the matter and now, for the first time, sent Chouet some documents. "All it took was a quick glance," said Chouet. "They were junk. Crude fakes."[9]

At about the same time—June 2002—a sometime Italian intelligence operative named Rocco Martino tried to sell the French a sheaf of documents reporting a secret Iraqi purchase of five hundred tons of uranium yellowcake. Chouet had them checked against the material sent him by the Americans. "The documents were identical." A great deal more might be said about these documents, which had already been passed to the British in late 2001, according to Bonini and D'Avanzo. The Germans, too, were given a crack at them. "The Germans asked our advice," Chouet said, "and we told them they were trash."

What is clear is that the documents, which were fabricated with materials stolen from the embassy of Niger in Rome, were given or at least offered to the British, the Americans, the French, and the Germans—all by the summer of 2002, when the US had decided on war to remove Saddam Hussein and was building a case that he threatened the world with WMDs. It should be noted here that intelligence services trying to bolster a weak case will sometimes pass a report under the nose of a foreign intelligence service to create an echo effect. Were the yellowcake documents the basis of British claims in an intelligence report released on September 24, 2002, that Iraq was trying to buy uranium in Africa? As "the dodgy dossier," that report—allegedly "sexed up" by aides to Blair—later became the subject of a major inquiry by Parliament. The British insist that they have other credible information on the yellowcake story but refuse to say what it is.

The Italian intelligence service concedes that its man—Rocco Martino, the sometime operative—was the one who circulated the

---

9. Carlo Bonini and Giuseppe D'Avanzo, *Collusion: International Espionage and the War on Terror*, translated by James Marcus (Melville House, 2007), p. 33.

yellowcake documents, but insists that he did it simply for the money. Bonini and D'Avanzo don't believe it, and point out that Italy's prime minister, Silvio Berlusconi, wanted a central role in Bush's coalition to fight the war on terror. A report in Rome's *La Repubblica* on October 25, 2005, says that Berlusconi pressured his new intelligence chief, Nicolo Pollari, to provide the Americans with intelligence that would inflate Italy's role.

Who dreamed up the yellowcake stratagem? So far Americans—public and Congress alike—don't seem to care, choosing to lump the Niger documents with all the other phony, exaggerated reports under the category of "intelligence failures." The yellowcake story didn't stand up for long, but it didn't need to stand up for long. An echo effect put it into play after Bush, in his 2003 State of the Union speech, included it in the list of scary signs that Saddam was preparing trouble for the world: "The British government has learned that Saddam Hussein recently sought significant quantities of uranium from Africa."

Tenet makes much of the fact that he twice blocked use of the yellowcake claim by Bush—once in September 2002 and again a few weeks later—but his argument was a narrow one: the president should not be a "fact witness" on the yellowcake story because the facts were too iffy. But not too iffy, in Tenet's view, to include the yellowcake story in the National Intelligence Estimate of October 2002 that persuaded Congress to vote for war. Nor did Tenet protest when the State Department accused Iraq in December of leaving the yellowcake story out of its WMD declaration, when Bush repeated the charge in a report to Congress, when Condoleezza Rice cited it as an example of Iraqi duplicity in an Op-Ed piece for *The New York Times* in January 2003, when Powell cited it a few days later in a speech in Switzerland, and when Secretary of Defense Donald Rumsfeld cited it at the end of January.

The yellowcake story would have appeared in Powell's UN speech as well if Powell had not drawn the line and tossed it out. That left the secretary of state with a lot of atmospheric intelligence rigmarole and two factual claims—the aluminum tubes proved that Saddam was going for nuclear weapons and the mobile biological weapons labs proved that he was a threat to the region and possibly the world. Powell's speech was all smoke and mirrors, but it was enough. Bush turned his back on the UN and prepared to go to war.

Hans Blix, meanwhile, had been undergoing a kind of slow awakening. Blix never answered reporters' questions about his "gut feelings" on WMDs, but he had them, and in the beginning they were roughly what everybody else believed—despite Saddam Hussein's cease-fire pledge to give up WMDs at the end of the 1991 Gulf War, Blix believed that he retained some and was trying to build more. But gradually the failure to find anything eroded Blix's confidence that his gut was correct. When the inspections resumed in November 2002, American experts suggested to Blix that the inspectors begin with Iraqi government ministries, seize computers, and look for names and addresses on the hard drives. Blix thought this a lame idea; the inspectors had tried it before, but the Iraqis were too sophisticated to leave incriminating clues in such an obvious place. "I drew the conclusion," Blix writes in *Disarming Iraq*, "that the US did not itself know where things were."

Between late November and mid-March 2003, Blix reports, the UN inspectors made seven hundred separate visits to five hundred sites. About three dozen of those sites had been suggested by intelligence services, many by Tenet's CIA, which insisted that these were "the best" in the agency's database. Blix was shocked. "If this was the best, what was the rest?" he asked himself. "Could there be 100-percent certainty about the existence of weapons of mass destruction but zero-percent knowledge about their location?"

By this time Blix was firmly opposed to the evident American preference for disarmament by war. "It was, in my view, too early to give up now," he writes. Tony Blair in late February tried to convince Blix that Saddam had WMDs even if Blix couldn't find them—the French, German, and Egyptian intelligence services were all sure of it, Blair said. Blix told Blair that to him they seemed not so sure, and adds as an aside, "My faith in intelligence had been shaken." On March 5, Blix on the phone with Rice asked her point-blank if the United States knew where Iraq's WMDs were hidden. "No, she said, but interviews after liberation would reveal it."

Two days later, Mohammed ElBaradei, chief of the International Atomic Energy Agency, in a report to the Security Council, decisively undermined the two principal American arguments that Saddam was illicitly pursuing nuclear weapons: the aluminum tubes which the CIA insisted were for use in a centrifuge to manufacture fissionable material were actually for conventional rockets, ElBaradei said, and the documents used to "prove" that Saddam was trying to buy uranium yellowcake in Niger were, in ElBaradei's diplomatic words, "not authentic." Only people paying close attention to the details understood at once that he meant the documents were fakes, fabrications, forgeries. ElBaradei's experts had reached this conclusion *in one day*.

In that meeting of the Security Council both ElBaradei and Blix reported their continuing plans for further inspections, and both said that outstanding issues might be resolved within a few months. This was not what the United States wanted to hear. In mid-February, President Bush had derided efforts to give Iraq "another, 'nother, 'nother last chance." Blix had pleaded in a phone call about the same time to Secretary of State Colin Powell for a free hand at least until April 15. "He said it was too late." But three weeks later Blix soberly argued in his report to the Security Council for more time. "It would not take years, nor weeks, but months," he said. France, Russia, China, and other council members favored the idea and proposed a new resolution which the Americans agreed to discuss but loaded with difficulties. "Nevertheless, I thought, here on March 7 there was something new," Blix wrote in his memoir, "a theoretical possibility to avoid war. Saddam could make a speech; Iraq could hand over prohibited items."

The resolution went nowhere but Blix did not give up hope even when President Bush flew to the Azores on March 16 to talk war with his allies, British Prime Minister Tony Blair and Spanish Prime Minister José María Aznar López. "Most observers felt the war was now a certainty," Blix wrote, "and, indeed, it came. Although I thought the probability was very high, I was also, even at this very late date, aware that unexpected things can happen."

Three years later, in a speech to the Arms Control Association, Blix reflected on that moment in his office at the UN—the afternoon of March 16—when the State Department's John Wolf called to say that the time had come to pull the inspectors out of Iraq. "My belief is that if we had been allowed to continue with inspections for a couple of months more, we would then have been able to go to all of the sites which were given by intelligence," he said. "And since there were not any weapons of massive destruction, we would have reported there were not any." An invasion might have taken place anyway, Blix concedes; the Americans and British had sent several hundred thousand troops to Kuwait and could not leave them sitting in the desert indefinitely. "But it would have been certainly more difficult," Blix said. Even so, in Blix's view, something important had been achieved. "The UN and the world had succeeded in disarming Iraq without knowing it." Blix guessed that Saddam hid his compliance so Iran wouldn't think him weak, but it was the Americans who were deceived.

That in outline is how we got into Iraq. When Tony Blair's UN gambit failed to provide an excuse for war, Colin Powell made the American case, putting in the scary stuff—the "product" of Tenet's CIA—which Hans Blix's inspectors had failed to find. No one paying serious attention was convinced. The French, German, and Canadian intelligence services were appalled by the weakness of Powell's case—what could the Americans be thinking? Periodically over the following year Powell would tell his assistant, Larry Wilkerson, that George Tenet had telephoned to say that the agency was formally withdrawing another pillar from his UN speech. "He took it like a soldier," said Wilkerson, "but it was a blow."

Tenet in his memoirs says almost nothing about UN inspections. The names of Hans Blix and Mohammed ElBaradei do not appear in his book. Tenet nowhere betrays genuine surprise that the CIA got everything wrong; maybe, he concedes, "reports and analysis...were flawed, but the intelligence process was not disingenuous." What shocked Tenet was the brutal manner in which the White House blamed him for the infamous "sixteen words," and even for the war itself, which never would have happened, the president's men implied, if Tenet had not assured them that the case for Saddam's WMDs was a "slam dunk." When Tenet read the phrase in *The Washington Post* he seethed for a day and then called Andrew Card at the White House to say that leaking the "slam dunk" phrase to reporter Bob Woodward was "about the most despicable thing I have ever seen in my life." Card said nothing.

Thus George Tenet broods about his hurt feelings. In the flood of his many parting thoughts he never returns to his original question about the moment when war became inevitable, which was in any case rhetorical. More to the point would have been answerable questions, the kind any fair historian would put to him: When did Tenet first hear the president talk about "regime change"? When did he realize that Iraq was next on the president's agenda? When did he understand that WMDs were to be the heart of the argument for war? And when did he know that without Curveball and without the aluminum tubes, Colin Powell would have been left standing in front of the UN with nothing?

—*The New York Review of Books*, July 19, 2007

9

THE REASON WHY

TO THE EDITORS:

Thomas Powers ["What Tenet Knew," *NYR*, July 19, 2007] does an admirable job as usual of analyzing the misdeeds and mistakes of US intelligence agencies. But in providing a scathing critique of former CIA director George Tenet's cowardly performance in the runup to the US invasion of Iraq, Powers fails to address the central question: What were the real reasons for the Bush administration's determination to invade Iraq and overthrow Saddam Hussein?

Powers dismantles one by one the planks in the administration's rationale (WMDs, alleged ties to al-Qaeda), but just mentions in passing another possible reason cited by an unnamed CIA analyst—"to settle old scores."

Independent observers have speculated on at least three possible underlying reasons: (1) the desire to improve access to Iraq's abundant oil resources; (2) the desire to improve Israel's security by removing the most powerful implacable Arab foe of Israel; (3) settling old scores, which could mean finishing the job the first President Bush failed to accomplish in 1991 by overthrowing Saddam, or retaliating for Saddam's alleged attempt to arrange the assassination of Bush *père*. (Admittedly, this would have the United States going to war because a son wanted to prove himself to his father, which raises the folly to a higher level still.)

It's clear by now that neither the facts nor any realistic notion of national interest drove the US invasion. Surely Powers owes us his best assessment of the real motives for war.

BOB GULDIN
TAKOMA PARK, MARYLAND

THOMAS POWERS REPLIES:

Bob Guldin in his letter raises an important question which the new Democratic majority in both houses of Congress has so far declined to explore. In the year before the war the Bush administration defined Iraq as a problem, and rejected every solution that did not involve regime change under American control following the invasion and occupation of Iraq. Guldin offers three possible motives for this insistence on removing Saddam Hussein while establishing a large-scale, long-term American military presence in the Middle East.

It's my view that all these motives—the lure of Iraqi oil, making the Middle East safe for Israel, and settling old scores—played a part, but none entirely captures the central idea in the minds of Bush, Cheney, and Rumsfeld. What's particularly odd is that there seems to be no sophisticated, professional, insiders' version of the thinking that drove events. Foreign policy professionals unroll the familiar story of worry about weapons of mass destruction, "intelligence failures," and dreams of democracy in the Middle East—a one-thing-led-to-another interpretation that relieves the administration of having to explain what it really had in mind.

My "best assessment of the real motives for war" suffers from the obstacle common to all assessments—none of the principals has been talking. But the fact that Bush, Cheney, and company had a

central idea seems unmistakable to me. Their determination to
invade and occupy Iraq says a great deal by itself. A useful way to
look at things is to recall the reaction in Washington to the Soviet
invasion of Afghanistan in 1979. Sympathy for the Afghans was several places down the list. What most aroused Washington, and
American allies in Europe, was the prospect that the Soviet Union
would keep on going to fulfill a longstanding Russian dream of
establishing a military presence on the Persian Gulf. The prospect of
that had policymakers like Zbigniew Brzezinski seriously worried,
because Soviet control of the movement of oil would provide a
mighty tool for coercion of the entire developed world.

What it was only feared the Russians might do the Americans
have actually done—they have planted themselves squarely astride
the world's largest pool of oil, in a position potentially to control its
movement and to coerce all the governments who depend on that
oil. Americans naturally do not suspect their own motives but others
do. The reaction of the Russians, the Germans, and the French in the
months leading up to the Iraq war suggests that none of them wished
to give Americans the power which Brzezinski had feared was the
goal of the Soviets. In any event, the planting of a large-scale, long-
term American military presence in the Middle East represents a
huge strategic initiative—a gamble, in fact, of the sort that makes or
breaks empires.

Just as interesting as the Bush administration's motives for going
to war is the evident wish of the Democratic majority not to know
what they were. How else to explain the failure to probe this question deeply? The Democratic majority is equally reluctant to question the drift of events now. All assume that the 2006 midterm
elections marked the beginning of the end of the American adventure
in Iraq. All favor some form or degree of withdrawal. But none to
my ear seems to grasp that getting out will take just as much resolution as getting in—and something else as well, which Bush has in

plenty: willingness to ignore the consequences. On this rock Democrats already seem to have run aground. The administration, meanwhile, shows no sign of abandoning its goals, and on the points that matter, Democrats seem to go along.

Three developments are particularly troubling—the administration's insistence that the surge is working but that Iraqi Prime Minister Nouri al-Maliki is failing; the growing tendency to blame Iranian "meddling" for military failures in both Iraq and Afghanistan; and what appears to be a changing of horses—back to the Sunnis—in midstream.

Consider the evidence of a policy reversal: immediately after the fall of Baghdad the US insisted on aggressive de-Baathification, in effect barring Sunnis from top jobs in the government and military. Now the administration is insisting that al-Maliki relax de-Baathification rules to bring Sunnis back into the government. At the same time the US military is creating battlefield alliances with Sunni insurgents, is encouraging the admission of Sunnis into the security and military services, and has remained silent while two separate groups of Sunni cabinet ministers have withdrawn from the al-Maliki government. It is likely that the US even encouraged the second group of defections by ministers loyal to Iyad Alawi, who has had close ties to the CIA for decades. Americans may not notice what is going on but the Shiites do. The obvious danger when the surge began in February was that we would bring the Shiites into the war against us. This now appears to have happened. *The New York Times* on August 25, 2007, reported the conviction of the military "that 78 percent of attacks against the United States are now carried out by Shiites." More remarkable still is the fact that a Democratic leader, Senator Carl Levin, has called for removal of the Shiite prime minister of Iraq, al-Maliki. Does no Democrat worry that a widened war with the Shiites of Iraq will bring a danger of war with the Shiites of Iran?

American political leaders, Republicans as well as Democrats, did not ask hard questions before voting for war in 2002, they have not asked hard questions about the president's goals in the five years since, and they are not asking hard questions now about the true nature and prospects of the bold imperial adventure which the White House PR machine insists on calling a "war on terror." I have thought from the first day of war that it would destroy two presidents—suck up all their energy and attention, while every other matter of importance was allowed to drift. Two presidents, I thought, because the second in the early flush of triumph at winning the White House would look for a new strategy to put off or disguise the reality of failure, much as Nixon did in 1969. Of course the new strategy would fail, and the new president would find him- or herself insisting that the new strategy needed more time, or that someone else—Iran perhaps—was to blame. The lesson of Vietnam is that it doesn't take long to get stuck. Not knowing why we went in allowed us to go in; not knowing why we should get out will make it impossible to get out. None of the presidential candidates seems to know why we are failing, or to understand what is imperial about the way we deal with Iraq, or to sense that a bigger war is just another mistake away. I don't know what we can do about this.

—*The New York Review of Books*, August 29, 2007

10

THE MILITARY ERROR

THERE IS A WORKING ASSUMPTION among the American people that
a new president enters the White House free of responsibility for the
errors of the past, free to set a new course in any program or policy,
and therefore free—at the very least in constitutional theory, and perhaps even really and truly free—to call off a war begun by a predecessor. No one would expect something so dramatic on the first day of a
new administration but it remains a fact that the president is the commander in chief of the armed forces, and the power that allowed one
president to invade Iraq would allow another to bring the troops home.

Barack Obama and Hillary Clinton in the current presidential
campaign have promised to do just that—not precipitously, not recklessly, not without care to give the shaky government in Baghdad time
and the wherewithal to pick up the slack. But Obama and Clinton
have both promised that the course would be changed on the first
day; ending the American involvement in the Iraqi fighting would be
the new goal, troop numbers would be down significantly by the middle of the first year, and within a reasonable time (not long) the resid-
ual American force would be so diminished in size that any fair
observer might say the war was over, for the Americans at least, and
the troops had been brought home.

The presumptive Republican candidate, John McCain, has pledged to do exactly the opposite—to "win" the war, whatever that means, and whatever that takes. Politicians often differ by shades of nuance. Not this time. The contrast of McCain and his opponents on this question is stark, and if they can be taken at their word, Americans must expect either continuing war for an indefinite period with McCain or the anxieties and open questions of turning the war over to the Iraqi government for better or worse with Obama or Clinton. Which is it going to be?

It is not just lives, theories about national security, and American pride that are at stake. Money is also involved. The two wars in Afghanistan and Iraq have already cost about $700 billion, and the economists Joseph Stiglitz and Linda Bilmes estimate that costs such as continuing medical care will add another $2 trillion even if the Iraq war ends now.[1] But the true cost of the Iraq war ought to include something else as well—some fraction of the rise in the price of oil which we might call the Iraq war oil surcharge. If we blame the war for only $10 of the $80–$90 rise in the price of a barrel of oil since 2003, that would still come to $200 million a day.

At some point the government will have to begin paying for these wars—if it can. What looks increasingly like a serious recession, complicated by an expensive federal bailout of financial institutions, may combine to convince even John McCain that the time has come to declare a victory and head for home. It's possible. But the United States did not acquire a $9 trillion national debt by caution with money. A decision to back out of the war is going to require something else—resolve backed by a combination of arguments that withdrawal won't be a victory for al-Qaeda or Iran, that it isn't prompted by fear, that it doesn't represent defeat, that it's going to make us stronger, that it's going to win the applause of the world, that the people left behind

---

1. See Joseph E. Stiglitz and Linda J. Bilmes, *The Three Trillion Dollar War: The True Cost of the Iraq Conflict* (Norton, 2008).

have been helped, and that whatever mess remains is somebody else's fault and responsibility.

Missing from this list is victory—the one thing that could make withdrawal automatic and easy. Its absence makes the decision an easy one for McCain—no victory, no withdrawal. But everybody else needs to think this matter through the hard way, trying to understand the real consequences of easing away from a bloody, inconclusive war. After six and a half years of fighting in Afghanistan and Iraq, the Democratic candidates for president and the public weighing a choice between them have a moment of relative quiet, right now, with the primaries nearly over and the nominating conventions still ahead, to consider where we are before deciding, to the extent that presidents or publics ever do decide, what to do.

The state of play in what some writers call the Greater Middle East is roughly this: 190,000 American troops are at the moment engaged in two unresolved hot wars in Iraq and Afghanistan. The magnitude of this endeavor is hard to exaggerate—two wars thousands of miles from home, covering a total area roughly as big as California and Texas, with a combined population of almost 60 million, speaking half a dozen major languages few Americans know. In addition, both wars are insurgencies, and in both the enemy is not a well-defined political, social, or military entity under central command, but something much more fluid. The difficulty of defining the enemy helps to explain why success, not to mention victory, is so elusive. In Iraq and Afghanistan alike the Americans have been trying to establish a government of convenience—friendly to the West, moderate in politics, predictable in business, open to peace with Israel, hostile to Islamic fundamentalists. The United States has been trying to establish such governments in the Middle East for sixty years.

What is new is that since 2001 we have abandoned talk for force. Our means are now military: the United States has sent its army to remake the social and political landscape of Iraq and Afghanistan, and perhaps of their neighbors as well. A long-simmering political struggle for hegemony in the Middle East has been abruptly transformed into a military conflict. The invasion of Afghanistan is easily justified by the Taliban's complicity in the terrorist attacks of September 11, but we must look for different explanations for the invasion of Iraq. That was a "war of choice" and it seems to have been prompted by two factors—sheer frustration with the long defiance of Saddam Hussein and American itchiness to use a military machine so superior to all others that some Army officers thought allies would only slow us down.

One big reason President Bush invaded Iraq was that he thought it would be easy, and in a sense it was. The occupation of Baghdad took only three weeks. But the formidable American military machine proved to be a clumsy instrument for conducting the political struggle to remake Iraq, and it has been powerless to prevent the growing presence and influence of Iran throughout most of the country. The fighting in Afghanistan has been less intense—five hundred American dead in six years, versus four thousand in Iraq—but equally erratic and frustrating. It is this shapeless military undertaking to remake the Greater Middle East—not simply "the war in Iraq"—that McCain promises to push through to victory, and that Obama and Clinton promise at the very least to limit and reduce if not to end. Let us look at these arenas of conflict and consider how things are going.

As soon as Baghdad was occupied five years ago things began to go wrong in a serious way. Responsibility for this failure can largely be traced to Secretary of Defense Donald Rumsfeld personally. He did not simply run an organization that failed; he personally made many of the key decisions that led to failure. As described by Andrew Cockburn in a useful new biography,[2] and supported by a five-foot shelf of other books and articles, Rumsfeld is a blustering, bullying executive

---

2. *Rumsfeld: His Rise, Fall, and Catastrophic Legacy* (Scribner, 2007).

with one idea at a time who dominated "planning" for the war. The one idea was to go in "light" with about a third of the forces the generals at first suggested, counting on a thundering opening bombardment—"shock and awe"—to cow the Iraqis while highly mobile US forces would dash for Baghdad. Once there, the army waited for further instruction, but the secretary of defense was flummoxed. He had no idea what to do next.

In particular Rumsfeld had no idea what to do about the storm of looting which began almost immediately after the Iraqi military disappeared and continued without letup until private businesses and government offices—the Iraqi oil ministry alone excepted—had been stripped of every movable item with a street value, from desktop computers and air conditioners to eighteen-wheelers. The US Army, ordered to stand aside, watched as the national infrastructure was carried away, a turn of events shrugged off by Rumsfeld with the explanation "Freedom's untidy.... Stuff happens."

While the Army was watching the looters it was not watching the vast Iraqi arms depots established by Saddam Hussein—munitions dumps covering literally hundreds of square miles containing among other things unimaginable numbers of artillery shells. It was these shells, lying unguarded and free for the taking for many months, that were soon being assembled by phantom opponents into deadly roadside bombs called Improvised Explosive Devices (IEDs). Rumsfeld dismissed the phantom opponents as "Saddam loyalists" and Sunni "dead enders," refusing to recognize the growing insurgency for a year.

When efforts to write an Iraqi constitution and create an Iraqi government elevated Shiites to power for the first time in many centuries, infuriated Sunnis responded with a program of sectarian murder. Shiite militias and their allies in the Iraqi military and national police in turn responded with an all-out killing spree that approached genocide—a campaign to push Sunnis out of mixed neighborhoods in Baghdad, and even out of the city altogether. At the height of the killing a hundred bodies a day were dumped onto Baghdad's streets, many showing signs of grisly torture. A million Iraqis left the country and another million left their homes for safer neighborhoods inside Iraq. By now there are two million refugees outside the country and two million displaced people inside. The man who had denied the insurgency now denied the danger of open civil war.

Rumsfeld was not merely wrong; he was self-replicating. The pattern of denial he established in the Office of the Secretary of Defense spread out and down, eventually reaching into the most remote crevices of the Office of Iraq Analysis of the Defense Intelligence Agency, where the young analyst Alex Rossmiller watched the DOD try to get what it wanted in Iraq by hoping, wishing, and predicting that it would happen. Rossmiller's memoir, *Still Broken*,[3] describes denial triumphant in both Iraq and the halls of the Pentagon. During his six months with the Combined Intelligence Operations Center (CIOC) based at the Baghdad International Airport, Rossmiller's job was to produce "actionable intelligence" on "bad guys" to be picked up by the Army. The job was frequently interrupted by spasms of bureaucratic reorganization and by VIP visits from congressmen who nodded through long briefings.

Those who worked at the CIOC—the FBI, DIA, and OGA (meaning Other Government Agency, which designated the CIA)—referred to it as "a self-licking ice-cream cone." By this they meant that the reports they wrote were read mainly by people down the hall, who sent back reports of their own. But eventually Rossmiller found himself in a Direct Action Cell putting together target packages which led to operations ending with detentions—actual bad guys taken off the streets. "Going after the bad guys," Rossmiller writes, "was at least doing more good than harm, I thought. But my optimism was misplaced; I was wrong."

---

3. A. J. Rossmiller, *Still Broken: A Recruit's Inside Account of Intelligence Failures, from Baghdad to the Pentagon* (Ballantine, 2008).

The lightbulb went on one night in the field when Rossmiller accompanied US and Iraqi special forces to help process detainees seized during an operation. Few details are provided of time, place, or occasion, but Rossmiller relates a harrowing, sixteen-page narrative of bullying incomprehension. The S-2, the Army officer in charge of intelligence for the brigade, explained the drill:

> Okay, we're going to bring in these shitheads on that pad over there, and then walk them over to this field. We'll put them on the ground and tag them, take pictures, and do a field debrief. Then they're off to Abu G where they belong.

Off to Abu Ghraib prison? At that point Rossmiller began to understand that all his care as an intelligence analyst to separate the good guys from the bad guys was academic. The debrief was a barrage of shouted accusations. What Rossmiller saw among the detainees was confusion, fear, despair, anger, humiliation, and tears. It gradually became apparent that one of the detainees, shouted at repeatedly, was a retarded deaf-mute. His brothers tried to explain this but were loudly accused of being insurgents and told they were "going away... for a long time." It was simply a question of paperwork. Two affidavits were enough to put a detainee in prison—one saying he was armed, a second saying he resisted detention. "They get an initial three-month stay," the S-2 explained, "and the debriefers there figure out what happens after that." Rossmiller got the point. There were no good guys. "Anybody who's picked up gets sent to prison."

That was Lesson Number One. Lesson Number Two emerged that autumn back at the Pentagon, where Rossmiller was a rising member of the Office of Iraq Analysis. In the months running up to the Iraqi elections in December 2005, Rossmiller and other DIA analysts all predicted that Iraqis were going to "vote identity" and the winners would be Shiite Islamists, who were already running the government.

President Bush and the US ambassador, Zalmay Khalilzad, publicly predicted the opposite—secularists were gaining, the Sunnis were going to vote this time, a genuine "national unity government" would end sectarian strife, the corner would be turned as the war entered its fourth year.

Rossmiller soon realized that this was not simply a difference of opinion. Nobody dared to tell the president he was wrong, either to his face or in an official report. This timidity ran right down the chain of command from the White House to Rumsfeld to the director of the DIA, ever downward level by level until it reached the analysts actually working the data. "You're being too pessimistic," they were told. "We can't pass this up the chain.... We need to make sure we're not too far off message with this." Some analysts protested and watched their careers sputter; most retreated into bitter humor. Reports were rewritten to support official hope. On the very eve of the Iraqi election a briefing was concocted to "report" that Islamists were worrying about a late surge by some administration favorite, as if a roomful of nodding heads at a briefing in the Pentagon were somehow going to carry the election in Iraq. Watching this exercise in magical thinking and self-delusion convinced Rossmiller that under Rumsfeld intelligence itself was "still broken" nearly three years into the war—an expensive charade to find or predict whatever the White House wanted.

But despite Rumsfeld's history of strategic and military failure, and the failure of the secularists as predicted by ground-level DIA analysts, President George Bush announced in April 2006, "I'm the decider, and I decide what's best. And what's best is for Don Rumsfeld to remain as secretary of defense." In November, following loss of control of both houses of Congress in the 2006 midterm elections, the president changed his mind, replaced Rumsfeld with Robert Gates, a former director of the CIA, and pushed through a new plan to stave off outright civil war in Iraq with a short-term increase of US forces by 30,000 referred to as "the surge." Now the surge is a year old and

General David Petraeus is pleased by the reduction in violence. But he recommends a pause in troop withdrawals next summer after the 30,000 have been pulled back. Has the surge achieved anything enduring? President Bush and Vice President Dick Cheney say they think so but the new president taking office next January ought to take a careful look at the rearrangement of forces on the ground in Iraq.

At the height of the sectarian killing in late 2006 it appeared that Iraq was spinning out of control. Senator Harry Reid, the Democratic majority leader, said the war was lost. Before the White House settled on the surge as a solution, national security advisers floated a number of radical ideas—dividing Iraq into three parts; dropping the democracy idea and backing the Shiites, who were in any event the majority; and leveling the playing field and bringing the Sunnis back into the government. In the event it was the third of these ideas that emerged during the course of the surge, beginning in the Sunni province of Anbar in western Iraq where the insurgency had reached its greatest intensity. There Sunnis who resented the Islamist fundamentalists of al-Qaeda in Iraq sought American help to drive them out. Modest pay of ten dollars a day, weapons, and a promise of eventual employment in the army or national police attracted thousands of former insurgents to join "awakening councils," now totaling perhaps 90,000 members.

Killing has been reduced, but the decline is the result of what amounts to American intervention in the Iraqi civil war. This new strategy was apparently adopted on the fly by the American military; it is working for the moment but it has dangers of its own. The councils, also called "sons of Iraq," are overwhelmingly Sunni in character. At the beginning of the occupation a key goal of the Americans was to disband the militias. In creating the awakening councils, the United States has armed, paid, and in effect sponsored the largest Iraqi militia of them all. But control of the councils is tenuous and they are now reported to be increasingly impatient with the Shiite government's refusal to enroll them in the army or national police as promised. The surge, therefore, has not so much ended the sectarian strife as it has set the stage for a renewal of civil war at a higher level of violence.

Iraq after the surge might be described as the same bomb, still waiting to explode, but with a longer fuse. What about Afghanistan? There the new president may find an even more intractable problem. In Iraq the United States is fighting an array of forces who live in the shadow of the Iranian sphere of influence, are mainly trying to kill each other, and are of two minds about American departure—some are reluctant to lose American protection, others want us to clear out so they can settle with local opponents once and for all. But in Afghanistan the United States and its reluctant NATO allies face a revived Taliban with the simplest of war aims—they want the foreigners to go. What is remarkable about the situation in Afghanistan—even astonishing—is that the Americans, after watching 100,000 Russians fight Afghans at great expense with no success for nine years, have signed on for a dose of the same. Lester Grau, a retired Army colonel, has edited three books on the Russian war using Russian materials, ranging from a general staff history of the war to small-unit combat reports.[4]

The implication of these books is not ambiguous. After their invasion in December 1979, the Russians walked into Kabul with ease, as invaders of Afghanistan invariably do, but after that it was mounting trouble all the way. The Russians paid a substantial price for thinking they could "win" if they stuck to it—a still-hidden number of dead soldiers, probably exceeding 20,000, and perhaps five times that number of seriously wounded; loss of nearly 500 aircraft including

---

4. The Russian General Staff, *The Soviet-Afghan War: How a Superpower Fought and Lost*, translated and edited by Lester W. Grau and Michael A. Gress (University Press of Kansas, 2002); *The Bear Went Over the Mountain: Soviet Combat Techniques in Afghanistan*, translated and edited by Lester W. Grau (National Defense University Press, 1996); Ali Ahmad Jalali and Lester W. Grau, *The Other Side of the Mountain: Mujahideeen Tactics in the Soviet-Afghan War* (US Marine Corps Studies, 1995).

350 helicopters; huge quantities of other equipment destroyed; hundreds of thousands of disaffected soldiers returned to civilian life back home, not to mention the opprobrium of the world.

The CIA officer Anthony Arnold, who was stationed in Kabul before the Russian invasion, thinks the penalty of failure went beyond immediate losses and humiliation to include the actual collapse of the Soviet state itself.[5] They were weaker than they knew, Arnold thinks, but the Russians did not give in easily: they killed more than a million Afghans, bombed villages to rubble, machine-gunned herds of sheep from the air, and drove as many as a fifth of all Afghans out of the country, across the border into the safe haven of Pakistan's Federally Administered Tribal Areas. Nothing worked and the war ended when the last Russian troops and trucks drove back across the Friendship Bridge into Uzbekistan in 1989. It is true that the mujahideen got plenty of material help from Pakistan, Saudi Arabia, and the United States, but it was the Afghans who fought the Russians to exhausted frustration, and have gone right on fighting among themselves ever since.

Shrugging off the lessons of history is the preface to disaster in Afghanistan. The Afghans seem so weak—an impoverished people living in mudbrick houses making a hardscrabble living; shepherds, farmers, and nomads answering to feudal lords ruling tiny villages connected by dirt tracks over rocky mountain passes. How tough can it be to defeat these skinny men in rags and occupy their country?

The Russians should not have been surprised by the answer. The British had already learned it the hard way before them—twice: in 1839–1842 and 1878–1880. Both efforts followed the standard pattern—easy occupation of Kabul at the outset, followed by rumbles from below and then open resistance leading to bitter fighting ending in disaster. It was the first of the British invasions that established just

---

5. Anthony Arnold, *The Fateful Pebble: Afghanistan's Role in the Fall of the Soviet Empire* (Presidio, 1993).

how bad a defeat in Afghanistan could be—an expeditionary force of 4,500, trying to escape Kabul, was attacked relentlessly on its way to Jalalabad. Only one man survived—the Army surgeon William Brydon. It is such object lessons that were ignored by the Russians and are now being ignored by the Americans.

The American economy, not the war, is the big issue in the presidential campaign as I write. The candidates have issued position papers on the war—both wars—and have adopted policies that can be summed up in a sentence or two. McCain wants to soldier on in both theaters. "Those who argue that our goals in Iraq are unachievable are wrong, just as they were wrong a year ago when they declared the war in Iraq already lost," he said in Los Angeles on March 26. "Those who claim we should withdraw from Iraq in order to fight al-Qaeda more effectively elsewhere are making a dangerous mistake." There's not a lot of detail here but there's not much ambiguity either: it's a tough fight but we can win it.

Obama and Clinton want to wind down the war in Iraq but focus new attention on Afghanistan—an approach that allows both candidates to draw on popular dislike of the war in Iraq while escaping charges of being irresponsible on national security. "We did not finish the job against al-Qaeda in Afghanistan," said Obama last August. "The first step must be getting off the wrong battlefield in Iraq, and taking the fight to the terrorists in Afghanistan and Pakistan." Clinton calls Afghanistan "the forgotten front line." Recently she added ballast to her own "plan to win the war in Afghanistan" with a nine-point strategy of sensible steps to invite more help from NATO allies and international donors while helping the Afghans to help themselves.

To walk away from the Afghans seems unconscionable; the country, poor to begin with, has suffered dreadfully with little respite since the mid-1970s. The Americans helped the Afghans fight the Russians and then turned away after the Russians left. The best account of the long Afghan ordeal leading to the terrorist attacks of September 11 is to be found in Steve Coll's *Ghost Wars*.[6] The focus is narrow—how the CIA managed the American part of a long, semiclandestine war and political struggle—but it captures the breathtaking seesaw range of the American way of meddling—ready with hundreds of millions of dollars to fight to the last Afghan one day, counting pennies the next, washing our hands of the whole bloody mess on the third.

It's not a pretty picture, but the CIA described by Coll was the one cold war presidents used instead of sending in the Marines; it made the same point, it was cheaper, and it could be called off without public humiliation. Now we're back in Afghanistan with an army and strong words about unshakable resolution, while the Pentagon cites worrying statistics about the enemy of the kind used to take the temperature of military conflicts. It's the usual stuff— a steady rise in small actions, ambushes, suicide bombers, attacks on convoys, clandestine traffic over the mountains into Pakistan.

The operative word is "more." The numbers are always inching up. NATO commanders have formally asked for three thousand additional troops. It's a modest number and suggests that the problem is manageable. The chairman of the Joint Chiefs of Staff, Admiral Mike Mullen, has remarked—casual words, not an announcement— that some troops withdrawn from Iraq might be sent to the "under resourced" war in Afghanistan. The presidential candidates disagree significantly about Iraq, not about Afghanistan. Nobody is talking about bringing the troops home from Afghanistan. We're committed.

George W. Bush is unique among presidents for his tin ear for trouble or danger. On his own he cannot distinguish between a notional or imaginary threat and one that is genuine, and his choice of advisers is no help. The big problem Bush saw on taking office was a threat by rogue nations to attack the United States with nuclear weapons

---

6. *Ghost Wars: The Secret History of the CIA, Afghanistan, and bin Laden, from the Soviet Invasion to September 10, 2001* (Penguin, 2004).

delivered on missiles. His solution was to redouble efforts to develop and build an antiballistic missile system. Rumsfeld and Cheney shared this priority 100 percent. Distracted by this technological chimera, which has eluded success despite huge expense for twenty-five years, Bush failed to heed clear warnings about al-Qaeda terrorist attacks. Later he was unprepared for Hurricane Katrina ("Brownie, you're doing a heck of a job!"), for the immense challenges of climate change caused by greenhouse gases, and for the full-fledged financial crisis precipitated by the lending practices of a runaway, unregulated banking system.

But these dangers were all at least new in some sense, harder to see in prospect than retrospect. This cannot be said for the president's decision to send American expeditionary armies to occupy two countries in the Greater Middle East. A better-read, more reflective man might have seen what was coming. Regretting adventures in the Middle East is one of the constants of history. The Greeks, the Romans, the Crusaders, the French, the British, and the Russians all sent armies and were forced in the end to bring them home again.

Invading the Middle East is the kind of imperial overreach that breaks the spine of great powers. Secretary of State Colin Powell tried to warn Bush against the magnitude of the undertaking with reference to the homespun "Pottery Barn rule"—if you break it, you own it. Did anyone go further and attempt to explain that Iraq was a seething cockpit of warring religions, political movements, social classes, and ethnic groups, many influenced by Iran? Did the president worry about the difficulty of occupying and rebuilding a country of nearly 30 million people with ancient scores to settle?

It appears that he did not. Going to war in Afghanistan and then Iraq was what the president wanted to do and he let nothing stand in his way. Afghanistan was not a hard sell but Iraq took real resolution. The arguments for war were weak to begin with and got weaker with time. The UN inspectors found none of the Iraqi weapons cited to justify war and asked only for some months to verify disarmament; the Security Council refused to pass a resolution for war; only Britain among America's most important allies joined the coalition of the willing to fight the war. But no setback cracked Bush's resolution and he went ahead. John McCain is content with the wars he will inherit if fate touches him with its finger, but Hillary Clinton and Barack Obama do not like the situation as they expect to find it. The war in Iraq promises only expense and failure, and the mix includes other daunting troubles—a Turkish military hovering just across the border from Iraq's quasi-autonomous Kurdish region, with one Turkish eye on the oil of Kirkuk; deepening connections between the Shiite government in Baghdad and Shiite Iran, which continues to ignore American threats of military action if it does not believably abandon its nuclear program; a safe haven for the Taliban in the Pakistani provinces bordering on Afghanistan; and loss of Pakistani support for American desire to take the war into the tribal areas. That safe haven made it impossible for the Russians to win, and it will soon obsess the Americans as well.

But set Afghanistan aside. Iraq is the big war. Getting out of Iraq will require just as much resolution as it took to get in—and the same kind of resolution: a willingness to ignore the consequences. The consequence hardest to ignore will be the growing power and influence of Iran, which Bush has described as one of the two great security threats to the US. Israel shares this view of Iran. No new president will want to run the risk of being thought soft on Iran.[7] This is where the military error exacts a terrible price. A political conflict transformed into a military conflict requires a military resolution, and those, famously, come in two forms—victory or defeat. Getting out means admitting defeat.

Is it possible that the new president will have that kind of resolution?

---

7. See Yossi Melman and Meir Javedanfar, *The Nuclear Sphinx of Tehran: Mahmoud Ahmadinejad and the State of Iran* (Carroll and Graf, 2007), and Kenneth Pollack, *The Persian Puzzle: The Conflict Between Iran and America* (Random House, 2004).

I think not; to my ear Clinton and Obama don't sound drained of hope or bright ideas, determined to cut losses and end the agony. Why should they? They're coming in fresh from the sidelines. Getting out, giving up, admitting defeat are not what we expect from the psychology of newly elected presidents who have just overcome all odds and battled through to personal victory. They've managed the impossible once; why not again? Planning for withdrawals might begin on Day One, but the plans will be hostage to events.

At first, perhaps, all runs smoothly. Then things begin to happen. The situation on the first day has altered by the tenth. Some faction of Iraqis joins or drops out of the fight. A troublesome law is passed, or left standing. A helicopter goes down with casualties in two digits. The Green Zone is hit by a new wave of rockets or mortars from Sadr City in Baghdad. The US Army protests that the rockets or mortars were provided by Iran. The new president warns Iran to stay out of the fight. The government in Tehran dismisses the warning. This is already a long-established pattern. Why should we expect it to change? So it goes. At an unmarked moment somewhere between the third and the sixth month a sea change occurs: Bush's war becomes the new president's war, and getting out means failure, means defeat, means rising opposition at home, means no second term. It's not hard to see where this is going.

We are committed in Afghanistan. We are not ready to leave Iraq. In both countries our friends are in trouble. The pride of American arms is at stake. The world is watching. To me the logic of events seems inescapable. Unless something quite unexpected happens, four years from now the presidential candidates will be arguing about two wars in Iraq and Afghanistan, one going into its ninth year, the other into its eleventh. The choice will be the one Americans hate most—get out or fight on.

—*The New York Review of Books*, May 29, 2008